Praise for
Awesome 'Possum
Volume 4

"An irresistibly vivid anthology of natural history and biology information presented in an appealing range of graphic styles. The delightful drawings and clever storytelling work with subjects from the familiar to the charmingly obscure, to offer an enjoyable learning for everyone."

—Dr. Ben Rowson, codiscoverer of *Selenochlamys ysbryda*, the ghost slug; taxonomist at the National Museum Wales

"After twenty-one years of teaching entomology, I find *Awesome 'Possum* to be one of the most educative, graphically accurate, and fun natural history series around. I recommend it up front to my students, whether for term paper ideas or escape reading at bed time!"

—Evan A. Sugden, PhD, entomology professor, University of Washington

"I have been finding that the snippets of wisdom I get out of illustrations actually stick as if someone had told me about them. That's because everything is so visual and is delivered in a way that is easy to digest."

—Anupum Pant, writer, *Awesci*

"*Awesome 'Possum*'s 200-plus pages are filled with comic strips whose eclectic styles mirror the variety of life they portray. On these pages dwell ghost slugs and bad-luck lemurs, parasitic plants and a bird with a shoe for a bill. It's biology broken down into bite-size stories packed with fascinating facts—ideal for kids and adults alike."

—Mike Shanahan, author of *Gods, Wasps and Stranglers*

"I love *Awesome 'Possum*, and even though I have been writing about this sort of stuff for much of my life, I learn new things on almost every page."

—Richard Conniff, author of *The Species Seekers*

"You'll witness love of the natural world with every story, and your own love for it will grow with every page. You'll learn stuff, too, and learning stuff is awesome."

—Jim Ottaviani, author of *The Imitation Game*

Awesome 'Possum

Volume 4

edited by

Angela Boyle

Awesome 'Possum, Volume 4
Published by Flying Dodo Publications

Content is copyright © 2018 each individual creator.

No part of this book (except small portions for review purposes)
may be used without expressed, written consent from
Flying Dodo Publications or the individual creator.

Flying Dodo Publications
ISBN 978-0-9970111-5-9
10 9 8 7 6 5 4 3 2 1   18 19 20 21

Editor: Angela Boyle
Design and layout: Angela Boyle
Heading font: Landsdowne by Paul Lloyd
Front cover inks: Tillie Walden
Cover design: Angela Boyle
Title page illustration: Elise Smorczewski

Flying Dodo Publications
Bellingham, WA
angela@flyingdodopublications.com
flyingdodopublications.com

First printing, August 2018

Printed in the United States of America.

Table of Contents

Introduction
by Jon Chad

One of the most divisive moments for me as a storyteller was in 2005 when I was rewatching the Fantastic Four film from 2005. There's a scene where Dr. Doom is pouring some sort of freezing gas on Mr. Fantastic (who has stretching, rubbery powers, for the uninitiated), and Doom asks Mr. Fantastic something to the extent of "what happens when you super cool rubber?" Dr. Doom leaves his own question unanswered, but pulls on Mr. Fantastic's finger, which only moves with great difficulty.

I realized two things in that moment. First, I realized that rubber becomes rigid when it is cooled. Second, and more importantly, I realized that the preconceptions that I had about the model from which you could acquire factual, scientific information about the world around me was far wider than I ever realized. My previous notions had segregated learning into a very limited spectrum of media; namely books and educational films.

What might be a beneficial way for one person to learn about the natural world might not work for another. We access information in different ways. Some of us need to see it all spelled out; the facts laid out as plainly as a census. Others need material that can connect to them across different literacies: visual, semantic, emotional, and so on.

The book that you are holding in your hands right now is a breathtaking example of this approach to education in practice. By using the language of comics, the artists in *Awesome 'Possum* 4 are able to communicate complicated ideas in a straightforward way that might connect to readers that have trouble with "more traditional" ways of acquiring information. And that's AMAZING!

Concepts such as time, smell, and taste don't need to be conveyed merely semantically in comics, but instead visually in new, sometimes unexpected ways. I believe comics can activate the reader's understanding of these intangibles like prose could only dream of! Nancy Canyon's comic on collecting bones renders the bones in such a way that I can feel their texture just by looking at the page. David Kirkham visually captures the smell of a grass snake so that it just oozes off the page.

The artists in *Awesome 'Possum* also expertly use comics to connect us emotionally to the natural world. There are some amazing stories about the human element in the natural sciences. David Humphreys asks us about the morality of zoos in his comic. Ally Shwed illustrates the boundaries that we've put up around us as humans; borders that has means nothing to the world of plants. Elisa Järnefelt challenges our own perception of nature and the "human filter" that we see the world through.

I've never forgotten what happens to rubber when you cool it down, and my sincere hope is that *Awesome 'Possum* will impart tons of lifelong fact to you that will spark your curiosity and appreciation of the natural world.

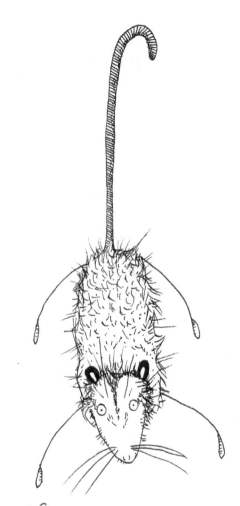

© Ej 2018
Elisa Järnefelt

Oh Boy, Can Opossums Find Food!

by Angela Boyle

Opossums, and marsupials in general, have been evolving since the dinosaurs.

And now they have adapted well to living well with humans.

They've survived because they're smart enough to remember where food is.

And they eat nearly everything;

in nature,

insects

berries

worms

frogs

fruit

small rodents

shellfish

and in more urban environments.

garbage

snakes

slugs

snails

birds

handouts

poultry

pet food

bird food

They have to eat year round because they store very little body fat.

Unfortunately for them, eating roadkill means they are likely to become roadkill.

Nancy Canyon

IF YOU HAVE A FRIEND WITH A LOT OF DIETARY RESTRICTIONS, GOING OUT TO EAT WITH THEM CAN BE TOUGH, RIGHT?

MILK

OH, YEAH... FINDING THE RIGHT RESTAURANT, AVOIDING ALLERGENS...

AND THE SAME PRINCIPLE APPLIES IN NATURE.

KOALAS HAVE ONE OF THE MOST HIGHLY SPECIALIZED DIETS OF ANY ANIMAL.

THEY EAT ONLY EUCALYPTUS LEAVES, WHICH FEW OTHER ANIMALS CAN STOMACH. TOO MANY TOXINS!

EUCALYPTUS IS NUTRITIONALLY POOR AND DOESN'T PROVIDE MUCH ENERGY RELATIVE TO HOW HARD IT IS TO DIGEST, WHICH IS WHY KOALAS SPEND SO MUCH TIME RESTING.

THE ADVANTAGE, OF COURSE, IS...

...THEY DON'T HAVE TO COMPETE WITH OTHER SPECIES FOR FOOD!

EXACTLY. THAT LEVEL OF SPECIALIZATION IS A DOUBLE-EDGED SWORD, THOUGH! IF ANYTHING HAPPENS TO THE EUCALYPTUS, THE KOALAS ARE OUT OF LUCK.

THE THING IS, HUMANS ARE PRETTY UNIQUE IN MORALIZING ABOUT WHAT THEY EAT.

AND THEY HAVE A TENDENCY TO IMPOSE THOSE MORALS ON THE NATURAL WORLD.

THAT'S WHY, WHEN YOU WRITE STORIES ABOUT ANIMALS,

THE VILLAINS ARE USUALLY "MEAN" AND "SCARY" CARNIVORES...

... WHILE THE "GOOD GUYS" ARE USUALLY CUTE HERBIVORES. LIKE ME!

BUT WHEN YOU SEE HERBIVORES EATING SOMETHING WE'RE "NOT SUPPOSED TO"...

WELL...

Tubey - deer eats baby bi...

OH MY GOODNESS, HE ATE A BIRD?!

Kami Koyamatsu

A Year in the Life

BY KELLY M. RICKER

KOALAS BREED SEASONALLY, FROM SPRING TO EARLY AUTUMN. GESTATION LASTS ONLY AROUND 35 DAYS.

FUN FACT

BECAUSE MARSUPIALS GIVE BIRTH TO THEIR YOUNG AT THE EMBRYONIC STAGE, A NEWBORN IS ONLY ABOUT THE SIZE OF A JELLY BEAN!

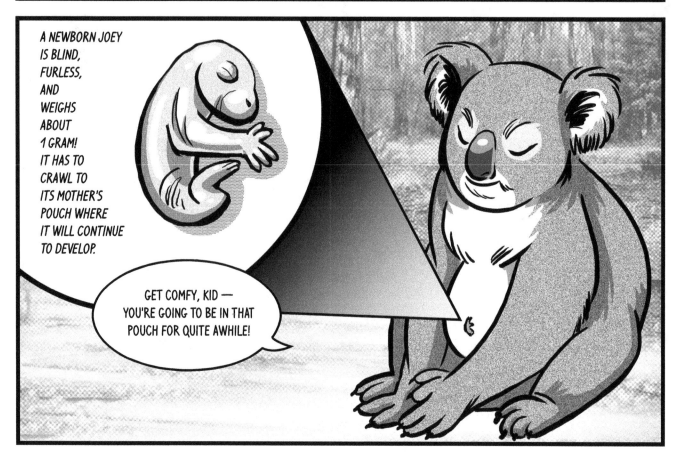

A NEWBORN JOEY IS BLIND, FURLESS, AND WEIGHS ABOUT 1 GRAM! IT HAS TO CRAWL TO ITS MOTHER'S POUCH WHERE IT WILL CONTINUE TO DEVELOP.

GET COMFY, KID — YOU'RE GOING TO BE IN THAT POUCH FOR QUITE AWHILE!

WEEK 7: THE NEWBORN'S SEX CAN BE DETERMINED.

A GIRL — I'LL NAME HER EMILY!

WEEK 13: FUR IS DEVELOPING AND EMILY IS ALMOST 2 OUNCES IN WEIGHT.

SHE'S GROWING — AND I'M SLEEPING! WIN-WIN!

WEEK 26: EMILY HAS ALL OF HER FUR AND IS BEGINNING TO PEEK OUT OF LORELAI'S POUCH.

SHE'LL BE MOVING OUT SOON!

EMILY HAS BEGUN TO PEEK OUT OF HER MOTHER'S POUCH TO FEED ON **PAP**, A SPECIALIZED FORM OF KOALA FECES. LORELAI PRODUCES PAP TO AID THE TRANSITION IN EMILY'S DIET FROM MILK TO EUCALYPTUS LEAVES.

MILK

PAP PASSES ON IMPORTANT MICRO-ORGANISMS TO EMILY SO SHE CAN BEGIN TO DIGEST EUCALYPTUS ON HER OWN.

YEAH, YEAH. DON'T JUDGE. CAN YOU PRODUCE NUTRITIONALLY BENEFICIAL POO?

DIDN'T THINK SO.

OKAY, THEY'RE NOT THAT CUTE. THEY'RE SORT OF ... LARVAL.

BUT THEY ARE AWESOME!

ECHIDNAS ARE MAMMALS, SIMILAR TO DOGS OR KANGAROOS, BUT THEY'RE A WHOLE DIFFERENT ORDER OF MAMMALS.

MARSUPIALS

MONOTREMES

PLACENTALS

ALONG WITH THE PLATYPUS, THE FOUR LIVING SPECIES OF ECHIDNA ARE THE ONLY LIVING MEMBERS OF THE ORDER MONOTREMATA, AN ANCIENT ORDER OF MAMMAL WHICH LAYS EGGS AND DOESN'T HAVE NIPPLES.

YEP. NO NIPS.

ECHIDNAS ARE NAMED FOR THE GREEK MYTHICAL FIGURE *ECHIDNA*, WHO WAS HALF WOMAN, HALF SNAKE, BECAUSE THEY HAVE CHARACTERISTICS SIMILAR TO BOTH MAMMALS AND REPTILES.

WHEN A PUGGLE BREAKS OUT OF ITS LEATHERY, REPTILE-LIKE EGG, IT LIVES IN ITS MOTHER'S POUCH AND GETS MILK NOT FROM NIPPLES BUT FROM TWO MILK PATCHES.

MILK: MAKES A BODY... PATCHY.

ECHIDNA FEMALES SORT OF SWEAT MILK OUT OF THE PORES IN THEIR MILK PATCHES.

THE PUGGLE SURVIVES ON THE MILK IN THE POUCH FOR ABOUT 1.5 TO 2 MONTHS BEFORE MOVING TO THE DEN.

THEN THE SPIKY MOTHER CHECKS IN ON HER DEVELOPING OFFSPRING EVERY FIVE DAYS OR SO TO GIVE IT MORE MILK SWEAT, UNTIL HE OR SHE STARTS EATING ANTS AND TERMITES OR WORMS AND LARVAE.

ALL GROWN UP.

BUT WHERE DO PUGGLES COME FROM, YOU ASK?

WELL, NO HUMAN HAS EVER SEEN AN ECHIDNA EJACULATE.

(BUT NOT TO WORRY! THIS IS A COMIC, WE'LL USE DRAWINGS.)

THE MALE ECHIDNA'S PENIS HAS FOUR HEADS, TWO SETS OF TWO, THAT IT USES ALTERNATELY TO IMPREGNATE THE FEMALE VIA HER TWO-BRANCHED REPRODUCTIVE SYSTEM.

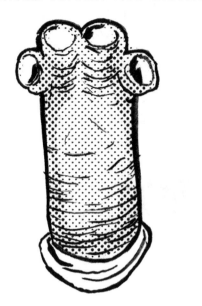
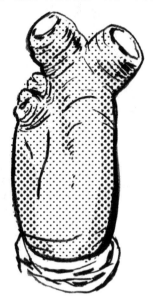

DESPITE ALL THE HEADS AND BRANCHES, ECHIDNAS ARE VERY ORDERLY WHEN IT COMES TO MATING.

THE FEMALES DON'T MATE EVERY YEAR, SO THE MALES LINE UP BEHIND A BREEDING FEMALE AND WAIT IN THE HOPES OF MATING WITH HER.

THE OLDEST MALE HEADS THE LINE, WHICH CAN BE UP TO TEN ECHIDNAS LONG, AND THE YOUNGEST IS THE CABOOSE. THERE ARE MULTIPLE LINES FOR DIFFERENT FEMALES AND SOME OF THE MALES ARE LINE JUMPERS.

THE FEMALE HAS
MULTIPLE PARTNERS.

THEN 22 DAYS AFTER THIS
COPULATING CONGA LINE, THE
FEMALE LAYS ONLY ONE EGG
AND PUTS IT IN HER POUCH,
WAITING FOR IT TO BECOME,
YOU GUESSED IT, A PUGGLE!!

WORDS: CAITLIN HOFMEISTER
ART: LAUREN NORBY

Tetrastigma rafflesiae is a native Southeast Asian vine, common to primary growth rainforests.

It is also a host for the parasitic flower—

Rafflesia.

SHING YIN KHOR

The flower remains invisible for most of its residency, growing as thin strands attached to the vine's cells.

When it finally erupts, it is difficult to miss.

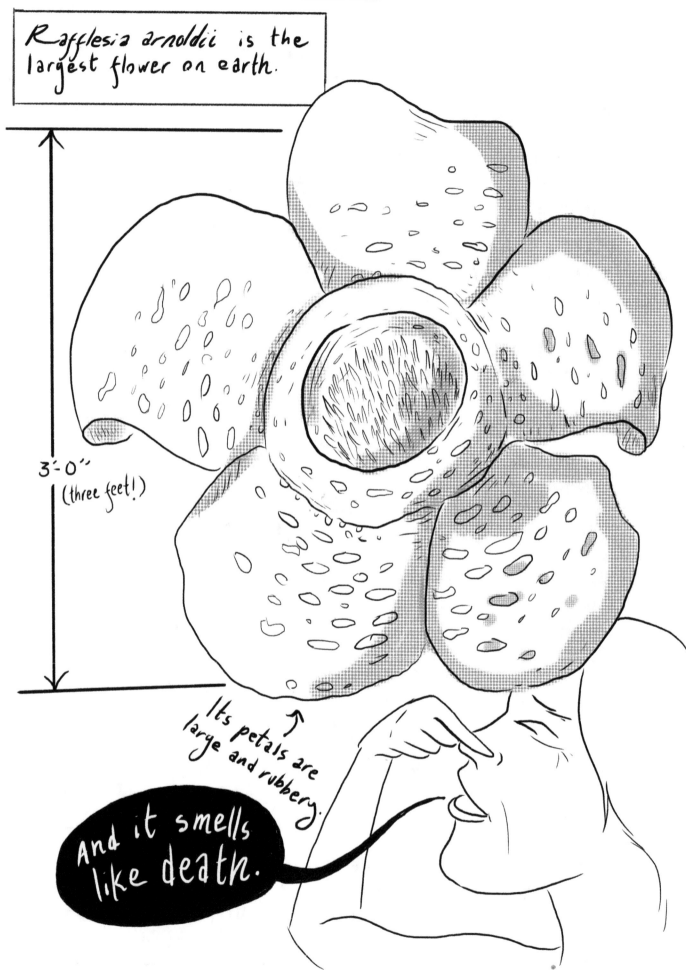

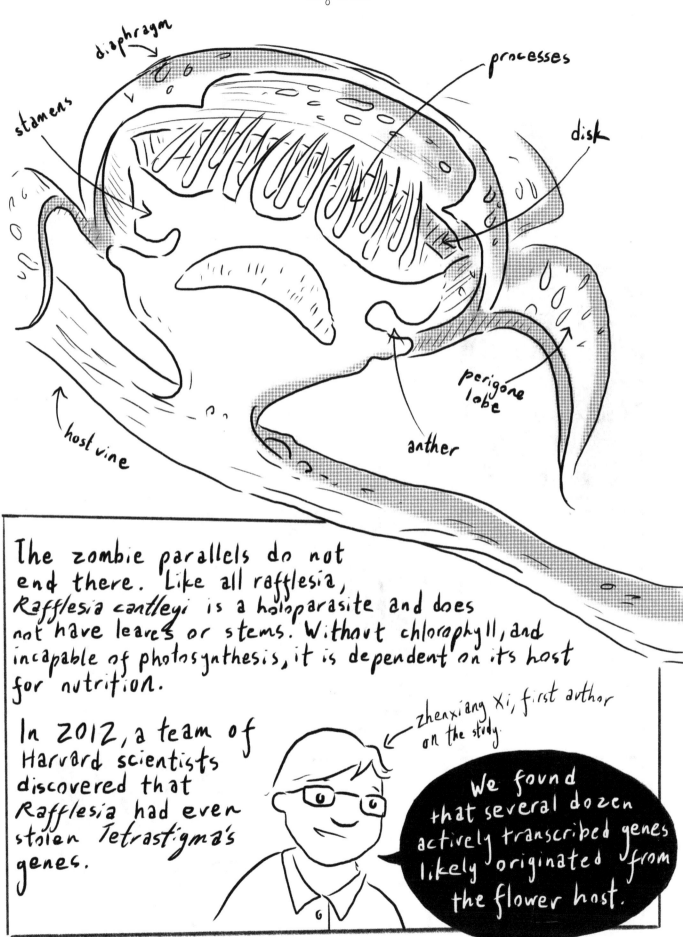

The zombie parallels do not end there. Like all rafflesia, *Rafflesia cantleyi* is a holoparasite and does not have leaves or stems. Without chlorophyll, and incapable of photosynthesis, it is dependent on its host for nutrition.

In 2012, a team of Harvard scientists discovered that *Rafflesia* had even stolen *Tetrastigma's* genes.

Zhenxiang Xi, first author on the study.

We found that several dozen actively transcribed genes likely originated from the flower host.

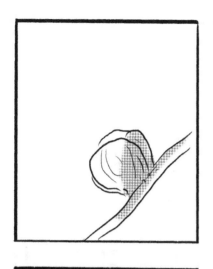 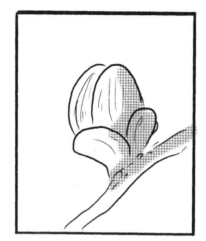 

still, the Rafflesia flower has a short life.

  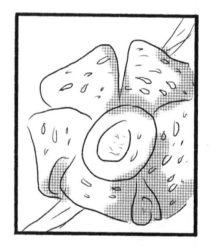

It blooms for just a few days

and then is gone.

The Shoebill

by Bridget Comeau

Shoebill storks (*Balaeniceps rex*) stand 110 to 140 cm (3.6 to 4.5 feet) tall.

The plumage is slatey blue-gray overall, with a darker gray head. The primary flight feathers are black-tipped and secondaries have a greenish tint. The underparts are a lighter shade of gray.

On the back of the head is a small tuft of feathers that can erect in a crest. The bill is an enormous structure ending in a sharp, curved hook.

The bill is yellowish with blotchy, dark spots.

The eyes are large and yellowish or grayish-white in color. The legs are long and blackish. The toes are extremely long and completely divided, with no webbing between them.

Shoebill storks inhabit the east-central part of Africa and are mainly found in southern Sudan (specifically in the White Nile Sudd), the wetlands of northern Uganda and western Tanzania, and the Bangweulu swamp of northeastern Zambia.

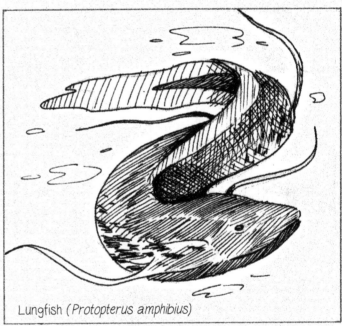

Lungfish (*Protopterus amphibius*)

Shoebill storks inhabit the freshwater swamps with poorly oxygenated water. This causes the fish living in the water to surface for air more often, increasing the likelihood a shoebill will successfully capture it.

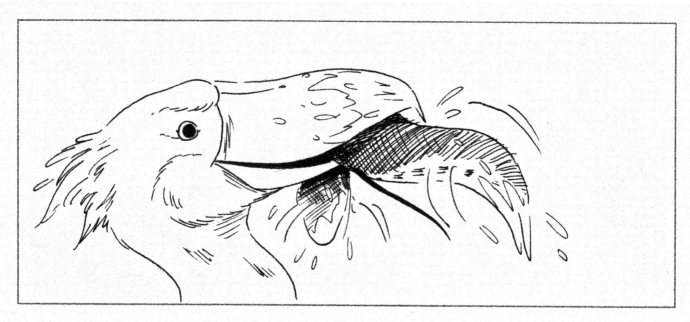

The taxonomic placement of the shoebill is a matter of some debate. It has traditionally been grouped with herons, storks, and ibises (order Ciconiiformes) on the basis of behavoral and morphological

However, other morphological and genetic analyses suggest a closer affiliation with pelicans (family Pelecanidae) and with hamerkop (*Scorpus umbretta*), another African water bird whose taxonomic position is unclear.

The composition of both the Ciconiiformes and the Pelecaniformes is, in any case, contested as well. Shoebills are sometimes placed in their own order, Balaenicipitiformes.

Shoebill storks are monogamous breeders.

Both parents participate in every aspect of nest building, incubation, and chick rearing.

A newly hatched shoebill stork is covered in silvery-gray, silky down, and juveniles are a slightly darker shade of gray then adults. The development of shoebill storks is a slow process compared to most other birds. Feathers do not fully develop until about 60 days, and the birds fledge at 95 day. However, the young cannot fly until about 105 to 112 days.

Shoebill storks are most threatened by habitat destruction. They have specific habitat needs for nesting and foraging, and their swamps and marshes are being rapidly converted to agricultural land and for cattle grazing.

The demand for shoebill storks in zoos is very high, selling for $10,000-$20,000 USD, making them the most expensive birds in the zoo trade. This price encourages native people to capture and sell these birds to zoos, reducing wild populations.

There have been few accounts of shoebill storks breeding in captivity. If they do breed, the young imprint on the zookeepers and will not go on to breed when they reach adulthood.

Steps are being taken in South Sudan to understand the population better and improve the satus of protected areas by raising local awareness, employing local people to protect shoebill nests which increases breeding sucess.

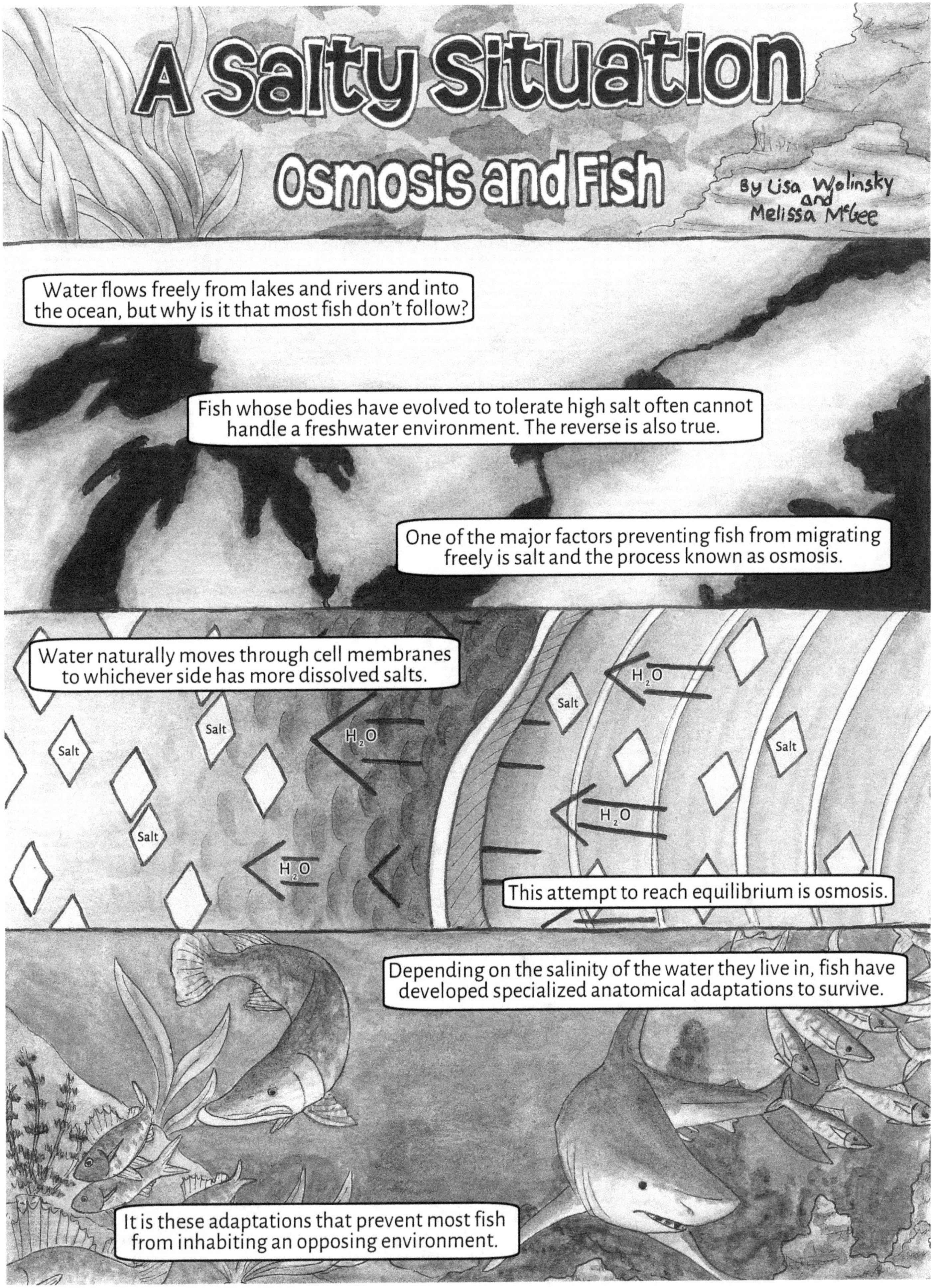
A Salty Situation
Osmosis and Fish
By Lisa Wolinsky and Melissa McGee
Water flows freely from lakes and rivers and into the ocean, but why is it that most fish don't follow?
Fish whose bodies have evolved to tolerate high salt often cannot handle a freshwater environment. The reverse is also true.
One of the major factors preventing fish from migrating freely is salt and the process known as osmosis.
Water naturally moves through cell membranes to whichever side has more dissolved salts.
Salt
Salt
H_2O
Salt
H_2O
Salt
Salt
H_2O
Salt
H_2O
This attempt to reach equilibrium is osmosis.
Depending on the salinity of the water they live in, fish have developed specialized anatomical adaptations to survive.
It is these adaptations that prevent most fish from inhabiting an opposing environment.

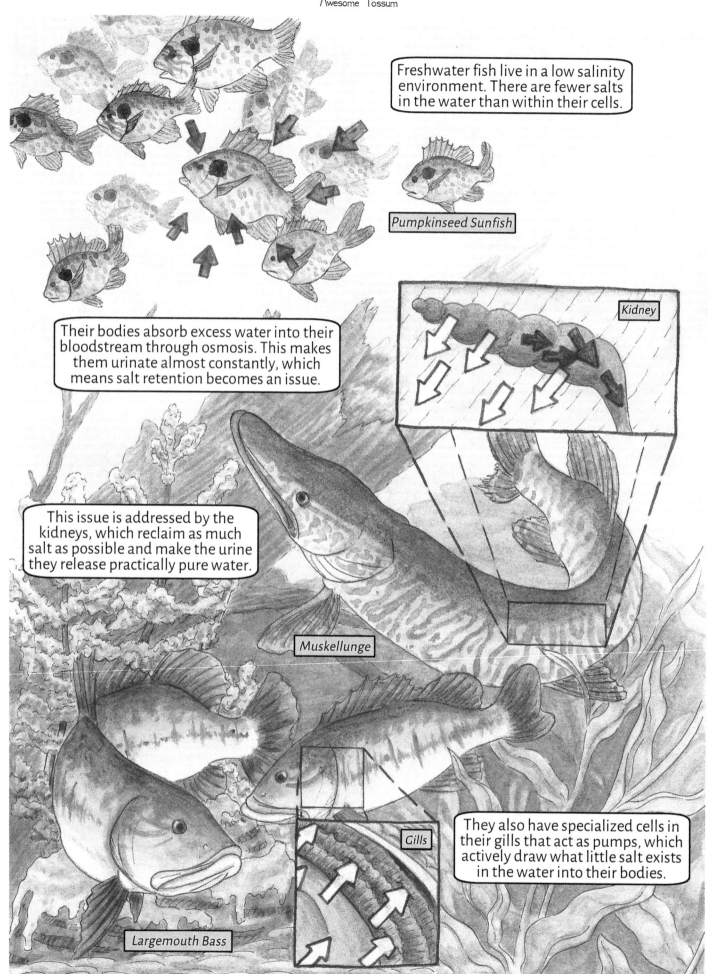

33

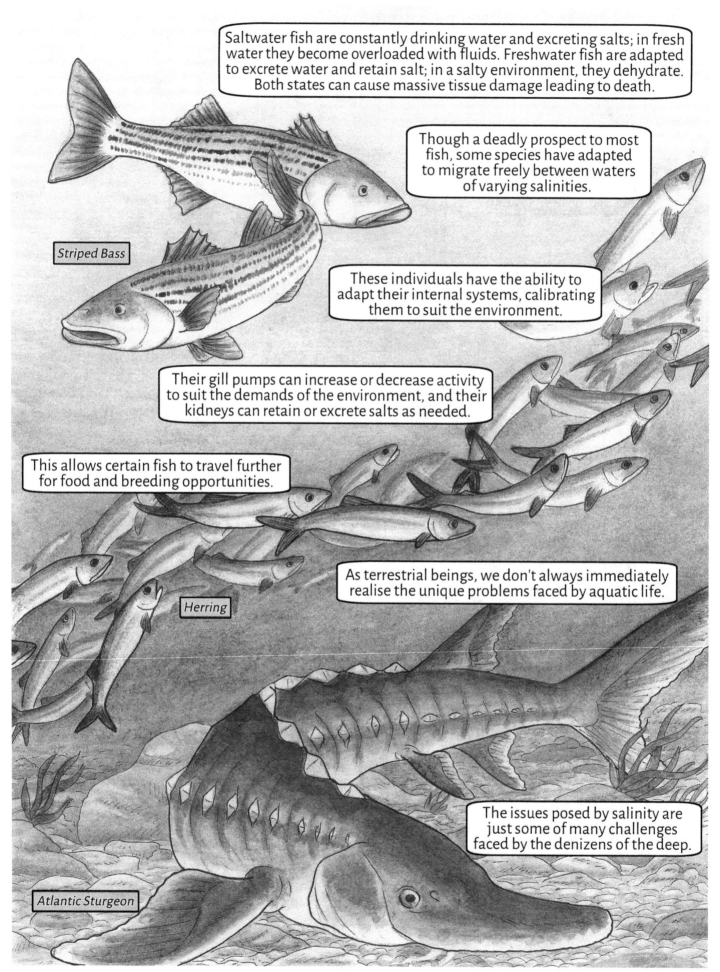

Saltwater fish are constantly drinking water and excreting salts; in fresh water they become overloaded with fluids. Freshwater fish are adapted to excrete water and retain salt; in a salty environment, they dehydrate. Both states can cause massive tissue damage leading to death.

Though a deadly prospect to most fish, some species have adapted to migrate freely between waters of varying salinities.

These individuals have the ability to adapt their internal systems, calibrating them to suit the environment.

Striped Bass

Their gill pumps can increase or decrease activity to suit the demands of the environment, and their kidneys can retain or excrete salts as needed.

This allows certain fish to travel further for food and breeding opportunities.

As terrestrial beings, we don't always immediately realise the unique problems faced by aquatic life.

Herring

The issues posed by salinity are just some of many challenges faced by the denizens of the deep.

Atlantic Sturgeon

Human filter  Elisa Järnefelt

Animals have instincts that affect how they perceive and approach their environment.

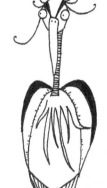

If a wolf spider (*Pardosa milvina*) is exposed to silk from its spider predator (*Hogna helluo*), it changes its manner of climbing on walls, increasing its chances of avoiding its predator.

Dogs' (*Canis lupus familiaris*) drive to detect moving prey is so sensitive that even a dry leaf flickering in the wind can kick off their hunt.

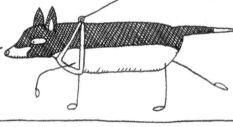

When covered by a shadow in an open space, striped plateau lizards (*Sceloporus virgatus*) either flee or alert other members of the population. They instinctively avoid both aerial and terrestrial predators that lay a sudden shadow over them when attacking.

Animals don't just perceive everything in nature.

They perceive the features of the environment in a way that is particularly relevant for their survival.

The world is dog-like to a dog,

and spider-like to a spider.

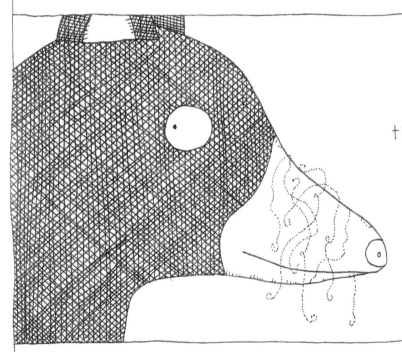

A dog can walk across the spider web without reacting to the silk that would make the wolf spider change how it climbs.

Similarly, a fluttering dry leaf that would excite the dog, or a shadow that would provoke a striped plateau lizard to run may not appear as anything particular to the eyes of a wolf spider.

Humans (*Homo sapiens*) often believe that they perceive nature as it is — objectively. But our everyday perception of the environment is as filtered as any other animal's is.

Similarly to other animals, humans have information processing tendencies that occur spontaneously and early in development.

No one has to teach a baby to notice and pay attention to human faces,

to make a distinction between animate and inanimate objects,

or to realize that objects have functions that can be manipulated.

As a socially interacting and tool-designing species, these are environmental expectations we form effortlessly as a byproduct of normal cognitive maturation.

These characteristics also skew the way we process information in adulthood and shape how things appear to us in nature.

When unfamiliar with nature, we intuitively draw on our understanding of humans and apply that to things and situations that we don't fully understand.

Plants eat their food from the soil by using their roots.

Green plants have photosynthetic cells, which contain chlorophyll and other light-sensitive pigments that capture solar energy. In the presence of carbon dioxide, such cells are able to convert this solar energy into energy-rich organic molecules, such as glucose.

We see human-like faces where there are none.

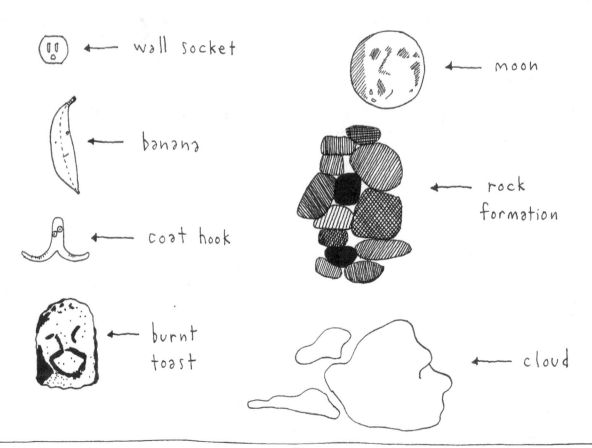

← wall socket

← moon

← banana

← coat hook

← rock formation

← burnt toast

← cloud

We constantly alter and shape our surroundings, and things in nature appear as tool-like to us.

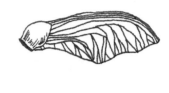

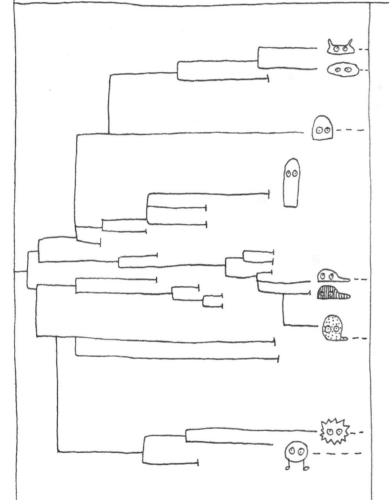

We easily understand natural phenomena as artifact-like: We expect that things in nature are purposefully made by someone to serve purposes that they seem to serve at the moment.

I love how the coloring of wasps is designed so that we know to be careful of them.

It's difficult for us to think that things in nature have come to be as they are through a constant process of evolution that does not resemble the creation process of artifacts.

Next time, while walking in the forest, or on the streets of your home town, pause for a moment and reflect on your instant impressions of your surroundings.

Think about what catches your attention.

Think about how it appears to you.

Think about how you understand its origin and functioning.

You will be one step closer to recognizing your human filter.

Ej 2018

40

41

FROGS & TOADS

NOW CLASS, WE MOVE ON TO PERHAPS THE MOST WIDE-SPREAD AMPHIBIAN OF ALL... **THE COMMON FROG!** *

CROAK!

*Rana temporaria

WHICH IS HOW I'VE BEEN KEEPING IT **ALIVE!**

·I FOUND THIS LITTLE GUY HOPPING AROUND IN MY BACK GARDEN!

YES, ALTHOUGH FROGS CAN BE SPOTTED PRETTY MUCH EVERYWHERE IN THE REGION, THEY HAVE TO RELY ON THE CORRECT LIVING CONDITIONS IN ORDER TO CARRY ON THRIVING!

FROGS TEND TO FAVOUR WARM, WET SPOTS SUCH AS GRASSLANDS, GARDENS, AND MEADOWS.

THEY ARE USUALLY FOUND BREEDING AND NURTURING THEIR YOUNG IN PONDS, PUDDLES, POOLS, AND LAKES.

MEANWHILE, THEIR COUSINS, **THE COMMON TOADS,** * TEND TO STICK TO PLACES THAT ARE DRY AND HUMID...

Bufo* bufo

...ESPECIALLY IF IT'S GOT **PLENTY OF** MUD TO KEEP THEIR SKINS **MOIST** AND **HEALTHY!**

CLARK'S JOURNEY WASN'T AN EASY ONE.

IN 1946 SHE EARNED HER MASTERS IN ZOOLOGY, AND IN 1950 SHE BECAME DR. EUGENIE CLARK BY EARNING HER PHD. THIS WAS A RARE AND DIFFICULT ACCOMPLISHMENT FOR A WOMAN AT THAT TIME.

DESPITE HER TRAINING AND INTELLECT, CLARK, ALONG WITH OTHER FEMALE SCIENTISTS, FACED DISCRIMINATION IN THE WORKPLACE.

WE HAD TO WORK EXTRA HARD... TO PROVE WE COULD KEEP UP WITH MALES...

CLARK'S HARD WORK LED TO MANY ADVENTURES AROUND THE WORLD...

...AND MANY IMPORTANT DISCOVERIES, TOO!

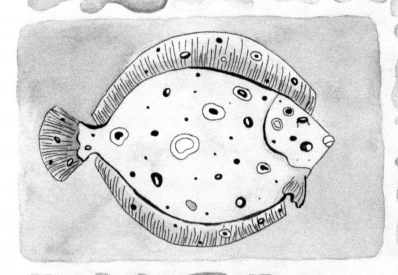

IN THE RED SEA, SHE STUDIED *PARDACHIRUS MARMORATUS* OR "MOSES SOLE," AND FOUND THE MUCUS ON THEIR SKIN IS A NATURAL SHARK REPELLANT. SHE FOUND THAT ANOTHER CHEMICAL PRODUCED BY THE MOSES SOLE BLOCKS THE POISON FROM SNAKES, SCORPIONS, AND BEES!

CLARK SPENT A LOT OF TIME EXPLORING THE RED SEA. IT WAS THERE THAT SHE DISCOVERED A NEW SPECIES OF FISH: *TRICHONOTUS NIKII*.

SINCE SHE DISCOVERED IT WHILE DIVING WITH HER SON, NIKOLAS, SHE NAMED IT AFTER HIM.

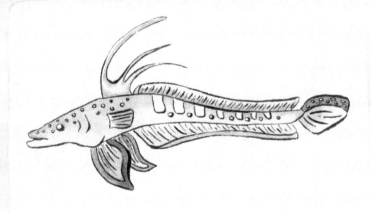

AND IN THE WATERS OF MEXICO AND JAPAN, CLARK OBSERVED REQUIEM SHARKS THAT SLEPT IN CAVES. THIS BROKE WITH THE COMMON THOUGHT THAT ALL SHARKS MUST CONTINUOUSLY MOVE TO BREATHE AND LIVE. IT WAS A BREAKTHROUGH DISCOVERY!

PERHAPS MOST FAMOUSLY, DR. CLARK TRAINED SHARKS TO PRESS SPECIFIC TARGETS TO GET FOOD. SHE OBSERVED THAT THEY HAD GOOD MEMORIES AND COULD LEARN TASKS AS QUICKLY AS MAMMALS.

PEOPLE GENERALLY THOUGHT THAT SHARKS ARE DUMB EATING MACHINES. AFTER SOME STUDY, I BEGAN TO REALIZE THAT THESE 'GANGSTERS' OF THE DEEP HAD GOTTEN A BAD RAP.

FOR MANY YEARS CLARK'S DISCOVERIES WERE MADE AT THE MOTE MARINE LABORATORY, WHICH SHE FOUNDED AS THE FIRST MARINE LAB IN SOUTHWESTERN FLORIDA.

This lab was much more than a place to do research. It was a place for the community to learn about sharks and other sea life.

This was an important part of the lab for Eugenie Clark.

Although Clark won awards throughout her life and wrote more than 175 scientific articles and several books, her work as an educator and an advocate for marine preservation and shark protection has left a lasting impact.

...I had a talent for communicating about the natural world. I came to see that it would be my life's work.

Eugenie Clark
(1922 — 2015)

Cute OR Deadly: Llama Edition

by Angela Boyle

"We're not cute. We're regal."

Everyone knows llamas spit.

They kick.

KICK
KICK
KICK

They even neck wrestle.

WOCKA WOCKA

But they do that to people only if they are overly socialized when they are young.

"Go away."

"I spit on you."

Verdict: Cute.

"Love me!"

Cute?

I'LL NEVER FORGET SEEING MY FIRST DRAGON.

WE'D BEEN TOLD BY FRIENDS THAT IF WE WANTED A GOOD LOOK AT THE SAN DIEGO ZOO'S KOMODO DRAGON, TO GET THERE FIRST—TO BE THE FIRST ONES AT ITS LAIR.

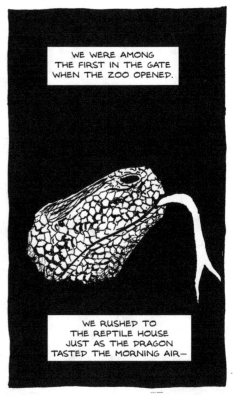

WE WERE AMONG THE FIRST IN THE GATE WHEN THE ZOO OPENED.

WE RUSHED TO THE REPTILE HOUSE JUST AS THE DRAGON TASTED THE MORNING AIR—

—AND STRUT OUT INTO THE SUNLIGHT—

—VARANUS KOMODOENSIS, SURVIVOR OF A MILLION YEARS OF EXTINCTIONS, ANOTHER MORNING IS YOURS.

SALIVA & SKIN:
SOWING THE DRAGON'S TEETH

©2017, 2018
STEPHEN R. BISSETTE (SCRIPT)
AND
ROSS WOOD STUDLAR (ART)

I CAN'T HELP BUT HEAR THE BOB & RAY COMEDY ROUTINE IN MY HEAD. BOB & RAY WERE BOB ELLIOTT & RAY GOULDING, AND BOB PLAYED "DARREL DEXTER, THE KOMODO DRAGON EXPERT, FROM UPPER MONTCLAIR, NEW JERSEY."

IT MAY BE A COMEDY ROUTINE, BUT EVERYTHING "DARREL" SAYS IS TRUE: "THE KOMODO DRAGON, WORLD'S LARGEST LIVING LIZARD, IS FOUND ON THE ISLAND OF KOMODO, IN THE LESSER SUNDA CHAIN OF THE INDONESIAN ARCHIPELAGO, AND THE NEARBY ISLANDS OF RINJA, PADAR, AND FLORES."

"WE HAVE TWO IN THIS COUNTRY THAT WERE GIVEN TO US SOME YEARS AGO BY THE LATE FORMER PREMIER OF INDONESIA, SUKARNO—

—AND THEY RESIDE IN THE NATIONAL ZOO, IN WASHINGTON."

THAT WAS BACK IN THE 1960S. THERE ARE MORE HERE NOW, LIKE THIS SAN DIEGO ZOO SPECIMEN.

THE FIRST ONE I EVER SAW WAS THE STUFFED AND MOUNTED TAXIDERMY SPECIMEN AT NEW YORK CITY'S AMERICAN MUSEUM OF NATURAL HISTORY.

THE FIRST PAIR OF LIVE SPECIMENS IN AMERICA ARRIVED IN THE EARLY 1930S.

ONE WAS EXHIBITED IN THE NEW YORK ZOOLOGICAL PARK—THE BRONX ZOO—IN 1934. THOUSANDS CAME TO SEE THEM, BUT THE REPTILES SOON BECAME ILL AND DIED.

KOMODO DRAGONS WERE CRYPTIDS, CONSIDERED ESSENTIALLY MYTHIC CREATURES, UNTIL THE EARLY TWENTIETH CENTURY.

THEN, REPORTS IN 1910 FROM DUTCH COLONIAL ADMINISTRATORS—

—A PHOTO AND A SKIN—RESULTED IN THE FIRST PAPER ON THE DRAGONS IN 1912, BY JAVA'S ZOOLOGICAL MUSEUM DIRECTOR PETER OUWENS.

ARTICLES IN NATIONAL GEOGRAPHIC MAGAZINE AND THE LITERARY DIGEST—BOTH BY W. DOUGLAS BURDEN, PROMOTING HIS 1927 BOOK DRAGON LIZARDS OF KOMODO: AN EXPEDITION TO THE LOST WORLD OF THE DUTCH EAST INDIES—OFFERED THE FIRST AMERICAN ACCOUNTS FROM THE JAZZ AGE.

IN SHORT ORDER, BURDEN'S MOUNTED TAXIDERMY SPECIMENS WERE DISPLAYED AT THE AMERICAN MUSEUM OF NATURAL HISTORY, WHERE THEY STILL RESIDE.

IT WAS BURDEN WHO COINED THE NAME "KOMODO DRAGON," AND IT STUCK. IT WAS HIS TWO LIVE SPECIMENS WHO SICKENED AND DIED IN THE BRONX ZOO.

Panels 1–3: To listen to the full Bob & Ray routine, go to http://bobandray.com/listen.html.

BY THE TIME BURDEN'S BOOK WAS PUBLISHED, THE LONDON ZOO REPTILE HOUSE ALREADY HAD TWO LIVE DRAGONS ON DISPLAY.

BY THE FOLLOWING YEAR, JOAN BEAUCHAMP PROCTER REPORTED HER OBSERVATIONS OF THE DRAGON'S BEHAVIOR TO THE ZOOLOGICAL SOCIETY OF LONDON.

SUBSEQUENTLY, THE DRAGONS RANKED HIGH AMONG THE MOST DESIRABLE OF ALL EXOTIC SPECIES.

PHOTOS FROM A BRITISH YACHTING PARTY INTENT ON TRAPPING MORE SPECIMENS APPEARED IN NATIONAL GEOGRAPHIC ("A MODERN DRAGON HUNT ON KOMODO," 1936).

IT WAS ALREADY EVIDENT HOW ENDANGERED THE DRAGON POPULATION WAS.

THE PROPRIETARY COLONIAL DUTCH GOVERNMENT OUTLAWED SPORT HUNTING COMPLETELY AND REGULATED HOW MANY SCIENTIFIC SPECIMENS COULD BE TAKEN.

WITH THE COMING OF WORLD WAR II, SUCH EXPEDITIONS GROUND TO A HALT FOR AT LEAST TWO DECADES.

THE MALE LIZARDS GROW UP TO 3 METERS—10 FEET—IN LENGTH, WEIGHING UP TO 150 POUNDS, DEVOURING ALMOST 80 PERCENT OF THEIR WEIGHT IN A SINGLE FEEDING.

THEY WERE QUICKLY RENOWNED FOR THEIR TOXIC SALIVA AND POISONOUS BITE.

LIKE CROCODILES, THE DRAGONS ARE CAPABLE OF RUNNING ON THEIR HIND LEGS FOR SHORT DURATIONS.

UNLIKE OTHER REPTILES, DRAGONS HUNT IN GROUPS—AND IN THE WORDS OF BOB & RAY'S DARREL DEXTER, "ONE SWIPE OF ITS TAIL CAN RENDER AN ENEMY SENSELESS."

IN HIS 1927 BOOK ON THE DRAGONS, AMERICAN MUSEUM OF NATURAL HISTORY TRUSTEE W. DOUGLAS BURDEN DESCRIBED THE LIZARDS' HOME AS—

—"A PREHISTORIC LANDSCAPE, A FITTING ABODE FOR THE WEIRD CREATURES THAT LIVED IN THE DAWN OF THINGS..."

BURDEN'S FRIENDSHIP WITH ADVENTURER-FILMMAKER MERIAN C. COOPER PROMPTED COOPER TO BRING THE KOMODO DRAGONS INTO A STORY IDEA COOPER HAD BEEN NURTURING—THE STORY OF A DISTANT UNCHARTED ISLAND WHERE WHAT MIGHT BE THE LAST SURVIVOR OF ANOTHER GIGANTIC SPECIES RULED...

...A SEMI HUMAN PRIMATE 'GOD' NAMED KONG, ITS NAME RESONANT WITH THE ISLE WHERE BURDEN CAPTURED HIS DRAGONS.

IT WAS COOPER'S NOTION TO SOMEHOW FILM LIVE GORILLAS AND LIVE KOMODO DRAGONS— PREFERABLY IN THE WILD— AND STAGE A BATTLE ROYALE BETWEEN THE MONSTERS.

"AFTER ONE OF MY CONVERSATIONS WITH YOU," COOPER LATER WROTE TO BURDEN, "I THOUGHT TO MYSELF, WHY NOT FILM MY GORILLA... THEN GO BACK TO YOUR KOMODO ISLAND AND FILM YOUR DRAGONS AND FOR THE PURPOSES OF THE PICTURE TIE THEM BOTH TOGETHER... GIANTIZE BOTH THE GORILLA AND YOUR DRAGONS TO MAKE THEM REALLY HUGE."

FORTUNATELY FOR BOTH ENDANGERED SPECIES—

—COOPER EMBRACED THE STOP-MOTION ANIMATED MODELS AND SPECIAL EFFECTS WIZARDRY OF WILLIS O'BRIEN AND HIS TEAM TO BRING KING KONG TO LIFE.

JUST AS IT HAD FOR BURDEN'S REAL-WORLD, LIVE KOMODO DRAGONS, THE BIG APPLE PROVED FATAL TO COOPER'S FICTIONAL CREATION KONG.

Panels 1–2: Quote from Mark Cotta Vaz, *Living Dangerously: The Adventures of Merian C. Cooper, Creator of King Kong* (New York: Villard Books, 2005): 194.

BUT *KING KONG* WAS A WORK OF THE IMAGINATION.

HUMAN ENCOUNTERS WITH THE KOMODO DRAGONS HAVE PLAYED OUT IN REAL LIFE—AND IN THE TWENTY-FIRST CENTURY, AFTER DECADES WITHOUT FATALITIES, THERE HAS BEEN AN ERUPTION OF DEADLY AND NEAR-FATAL ATTACKS.

A DRAGON KILLED AN 8-YEAR-OLD BOY ON KOMODO ISLAND IN 2007, THE FIRST HUMAN DEATH-BY-DRAGON IN 33 YEARS.

WESOME 'POSSUM EN'S ADVENTURE

DRAGONS TORE MY FLESH

ONE YEAR LATER, SCUBA DIVERS SPENT OVER TEN HOURS ADRIFT UNTIL BEACHING ON RINCA ISLAND—25 MILES FROM THEIR BOAT—WHERE A POPULATION OF 1,300 DRAGONS DWELL.

THE DESPERATE DIVERS FOUGHT OFF RAVENOUS DRAGONS AND THE ELEMENTS FOR TWO DAYS AND TWO NIGHTS, UNTIL AN INDONESIAN RESCUE CREW SAVED THEIR LIVES AND SPED THEM TO THE LOCAL HOSPITAL ON FLORES ISLAND.

THANKFULLY, ALL SURVIVED.

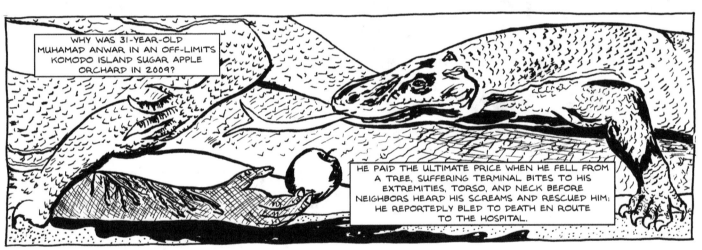

WHY WAS 31-YEAR-OLD MUHAMAD ANWAR IN AN OFF-LIMITS KOMODO ISLAND SUGAR APPLE ORCHARD IN 2009?

HE PAID THE ULTIMATE PRICE WHEN HE FELL FROM A TREE, SUFFERING TERMINAL BITES TO HIS EXTREMITIES, TORSO, AND NECK BEFORE NEIGHBORS HEARD HIS SCREAMS AND RESCUED HIM; HE REPORTEDLY BLED TO DEATH EN ROUTE TO THE HOSPITAL.

FAR MORE FORTUNATE WAS A FELLOW IN 2009, NAMED MAEN, WHO WORKED ON RINCA ISLAND. MAEN MANAGED TO PRY OPEN THE JAWS OF A KOMODO DRAGON THAT HAD CREPT INTO HIS OFFICE AND SEIZED HIS LEG.

MAEN WAS FLOWN TO BALI FOR A SIX-HOUR SURGERY, REQUIRING 55 STITCHES AND SIX MONTHS TO RECOVER... BUT HE DID SURVIVE.

A SIMILAR INCIDENT OCCURRED IN 2001 IN THE LOS ANGELES ZOO, WHERE INVESTIGATIVE JOURNALIST PHIL BRONSTEIN ALMOST LOST HIS FOOT TO A KOMODO DRAGON DURING A PRE-ARRANGED PHOTO SHOOT WITH THE DRAGON—

—A BIRTHDAY GIFT ARRANGED BY BRONSTEIN'S WIFE. HE WAS MARRIED AT THAT TIME TO ACTRESS SHARON STONE. APPARENTLY NO ONE EXPECTED THE DRAGON'S BASIC INSTINCT TO ASSERT ITSELF.

BRONSTEIN SURVIVED THE INCIDENT AND DID NOT PRESS CHARGES.

Panel 1: Fred Attwell, "Boy Killed in Dragon Attack," *The Guardian*, June 4 2007, https://www.theguardian.com/world/2007/jun/04/1.

Panel 2: Richard Edwards, "Stranded Divers Had to Fight Off Komodo Dragons to Survive," *The Telegraph*, June 8, 2008, http://www.telegraph.co.uk/news/worldnews/asia/indonesia/2095835/Stranded-divers-had-to-fight-off-Komodo-dragons-to-survive.html.

Panel 3: Stephen Bates, "Komodo Dragons Maul Man to Death," *The Guardian*, March 24, 2009, https://www.theguardian.com/world/2009/mar/24/man-mauled-death-komodo-dragon; Barry Neild, "Komodo Dragons Kill Indonesian Fisherman," CNN, March 24, 2009. http://edition.cnn.com/2009/WORLD/asiapcf/03/24/komodo.dragon.

Panel 4: Michael Turtle, "I Was Attached by a Dragon and Survived," *Time Travel Turtle*, last accessed February 24, 2018, https://www.timetravelturtle.com/attack-komodo-dragon-indonesia; Irwan Firdaus, "Komodo Dragon Attacks Terrorize Villages," NBC, May 24, 2009, http://www.nbcnews.com/id/30913500/ns/technology_and_science-science/t/komodo-dragon-attacks-terrorize-villages/#.UP1rW6F2F28.

Panel 5: Jess Cage, "Transcript: Sharon Stone vs. the Komodo Dragon," *Time*, June 23, 2001, http://content.time.com/time/arts/article/0,8599,133163,00.html.

WE SAW OUR LIVING KOMODO DRAGON YEARS EARLIER AND ABOUT 130 MILES SOUTH OF WHERE BRONSTEIN WAS ATTACKED.

ITS SCALY HIDE SEEMED A DULL GRAY-BROWN IN COLOR, UNLESS YOU LOOKED VERY CLOSELY AT THE MULTI-COLORED SCALES.

WE WATCHED UNTIL IT RETURNED TO ITS MAN-MADE DEN. IT HID FROM SIGHT THE REST OF THE TIME WE WERE THERE.

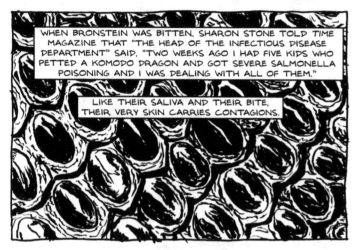

WHEN BRONSTEIN WAS BITTEN, SHARON STONE TOLD TIME MAGAZINE THAT "THE HEAD OF THE INFECTIOUS DISEASE DEPARTMENT" SAID, "TWO WEEKS AGO I HAD FIVE KIDS WHO PETTED A KOMODO DRAGON AND GOT SEVERE SALMONELLA POISONING AND I WAS DEALING WITH ALL OF THEM."

LIKE THEIR SALIVA AND THEIR BITE, THEIR VERY SKIN CARRIES CONTAGIONS.

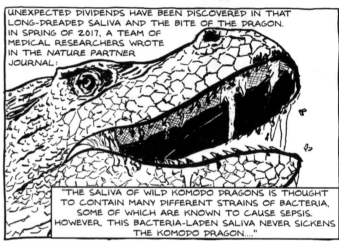

UNEXPECTED DIVIDENDS HAVE BEEN DISCOVERED IN THAT LONG-DREADED SALIVA AND THE BITE OF THE DRAGON. IN SPRING OF 2017, A TEAM OF MEDICAL RESEARCHERS WROTE IN THE NATURE PARTNER JOURNAL:

"THE SALIVA OF WILD KOMODO DRAGONS IS THOUGHT TO CONTAIN MANY DIFFERENT STRAINS OF BACTERIA, SOME OF WHICH ARE KNOWN TO CAUSE SEPSIS. HOWEVER, THIS BACTERIA-LADEN SALIVA NEVER SICKENS THE KOMODO DRAGON...."

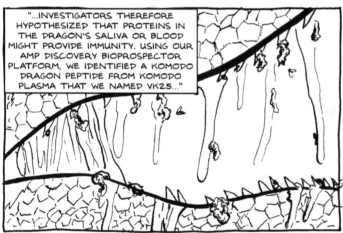

"...INVESTIGATORS THEREFORE HYPOTHESIZED THAT PROTEINS IN THE DRAGON'S SALIVA OR BLOOD MIGHT PROVIDE IMMUNITY. USING OUR AMP DISCOVERY BIOPROSPECTOR PLATFORM, WE IDENTIFIED A KOMODO DRAGON PEPTIDE FROM KOMODO PLASMA THAT WE NAMED VK25..."

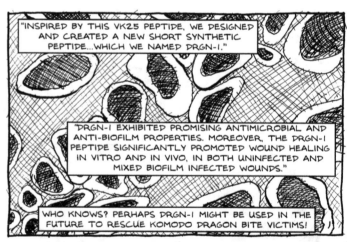

"INSPIRED BY THIS VK25 PEPTIDE, WE DESIGNED AND CREATED A NEW SHORT SYNTHETIC PEPTIDE...WHICH WE NAMED DRGN-1."

"DRGN-1 EXHIBITED PROMISING ANTIMICROBIAL AND ANTI-BIOFILM PROPERTIES. MOREOVER, THE DRGN-1 PEPTIDE SIGNIFICANTLY PROMOTED WOUND HEALING IN VITRO AND IN VIVO, IN BOTH UNINFECTED AND MIXED BIOFILM INFECTED WOUNDS."

WHO KNOWS? PERHAPS DRGN-1 MIGHT BE USED IN THE FUTURE TO RESCUE KOMODO DRAGON BITE VICTIMS!

LATER IN 2017—90 YEARS AFTER THE SPECIES WAS FIRST CAPTURED AND EXHIBITED IN THE LONDON ZOO—A THANKSGIVING WEEKEND SURPRISE EMERGED IN FORT WORTH, TEXAS.

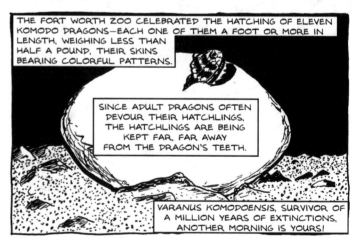

THE FORT WORTH ZOO CELEBRATED THE HATCHING OF ELEVEN KOMODO DRAGONS—EACH ONE OF THEM A FOOT OR MORE IN LENGTH, WEIGHING LESS THAN HALF A POUND, THEIR SKINS BEARING COLORFUL PATTERNS.

SINCE ADULT DRAGONS OFTEN DEVOUR THEIR HATCHLINGS, THE HATCHLINGS ARE BEING KEPT FAR, FAR AWAY FROM THE DRAGON'S TEETH.

VARANUS KOMODOENSIS, SURVIVOR OF A MILLION YEARS OF EXTINCTIONS, ANOTHER MORNING IS YOURS!

Panels 3–5: Quoted from Ezra M. C. Chung, Scott N. Dean, Crystal N. Propst, Barney M. Bishop, and Monique L. van Hoek, "Komodo Dragon-Inspired Synthetic Peptide DRGN-1 Promotes Wound-Healing of a Mixed-Biofilm Infected Wound," Ezra M.C. Chung, Scott N. Dean, Crystal N. Propst, Barney M. Bishop & Monique L. van Hoek, *Nature Partner Journal: Biofilms and Microbiomes* 3, no. 1 (April 11, 2017): 9, doi: 10.1038/s41522-017-0017-2.

HELLO!
I'M A BEAR IN A SUIT.

HUMANS HAVE PUT ANIMALS IN CAGES FOR EDUCATION AND ENTERTAINMENT FOR AT LEAST **5,000 YEARS.**

LATELY, THEY'VE GOTTEN A LOT BETTER AT IT.

BUT IS IT ENOUGH?

LET'S START HERE —
IT'S COMPLICATED.

AND WE'RE JUST BARELY GOING TO SCRATCH THE SURFACE.

ZOOS HELP PEOPLE SEE ANIMALS UP CLOSE AND PERSONAL, AND THAT'S A MAGICAL THING.

BUT DEPENDING ON HOW MUCH EMPATHY YOU HAVE FOR ANIMALS, ZOOS CAN ALSO BE FOR-PROFIT INTERNMENT CAMPS.

Are **ZOOS** a Good Idea?

BY DAVID HUMPHREYS • @DBHUM

conservation and education

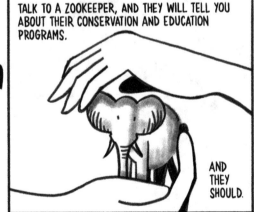

TALK TO A ZOOKEEPER, AND THEY WILL TELL YOU ABOUT THEIR CONSERVATION AND EDUCATION PROGRAMS.

AND THEY SHOULD.

WELL-DESIGNED ZOOS CAN PLAY AN IMPORTANT EDUCATIONAL ROLE, AND EXPOSURE TO AN ANIMAL IN REAL LIFE CAN BE A TRANSFORMATIONAL EXPERIENCE, ESPECIALLY FOR CHILDREN.

ADDITIONALLY, ZOOS ARE TRAILBLAZERS IN CONSERVATION EFFORTS. IN 2017, MEMBERS OF THE AZA* GAVE OVER $200 MILLION DOLLARS TO WILDLIFE CONSERVATION.

* ASSOCIATION OF ZOOS AND AQUARIUMS

ZOOS HAVE HELPED RESTORE ENDANGERED ANIMALS TO THE WILD.

CALIFORNIA CONDOR

PRZEWALSKI'S HORSE

PÈRE DAVID'S DEER

— AND MANY OTHERS!

AND SOME ZOOS ARE JUST CRAZY **BEAUTIFUL**

HOW WOULD YOU KNOW THE POWER AND SPEED OF A RHINO IF IT WEREN'T FOR A GOOD ZOO?

RUNNING A SUCCESSFUL ZOO IS RUNNING A SUCCESSFUL BUSINESS. THE OWNERS HAVE TO BALANCE COSTS AGAINST PROFITS.

But — a zoo is a business.

EXPENSE   INCOME

AS A RESULT, ZOOS TEND TO BE OPTIMIZED FOR HUMANS AND NOT FOR ANIMALS.

IDEALLY IT'D BE BOTH, OF COURSE. BUT MONEY IS ALWAYS SHORT.

OR TO PUT IT ANOTHER WAY, ANIMALS HAVE THEIR BASIC FREEDOMS TAKEN AND THEN ARE USED AS COMMODITIES TO LINE HUMAN POCKETS.

FREE

SLAVE

Zoos trade on the freedom of animals.

ZOO PEOPLE WILL SAY THAT "ANIMALS IN CAPTIVITY ARE SAFE AND COMFORTABLE AND BETTER OFF."

AND CAPTIVITY IS EASIER FOR SOME ANIMALS THAN IT IS FOR OTHERS.

THESE FLAMINGOS DON'T LET A CAGE GET IN THE WAY OF A GOOD TIME.

BUT, IN GENERAL, THE LESS AN ANIMAL CAN DO ITS NATURAL BEHAVIORS, THE LESS HAPPY IT IS.

DREAMS OF RUNNING   DREAMS OF MATING   DREAMS OF HUNTING PREY

UNHAPPY ZOO ANIMALS MIGHT ENGAGE IN VARIOUS IRRATIONAL BEHAVIORS CALLED "ZOOCHOSIS."

PACING ROCKING PULLING OUT HAIR

Are zoos just creepy?

IS THE BASIC PREMISE OF A ZOO **A GOOD IDEA?**

IS KEEPING AN INTELLIGENT ANIMAL IN A CAGE **MORAL?**

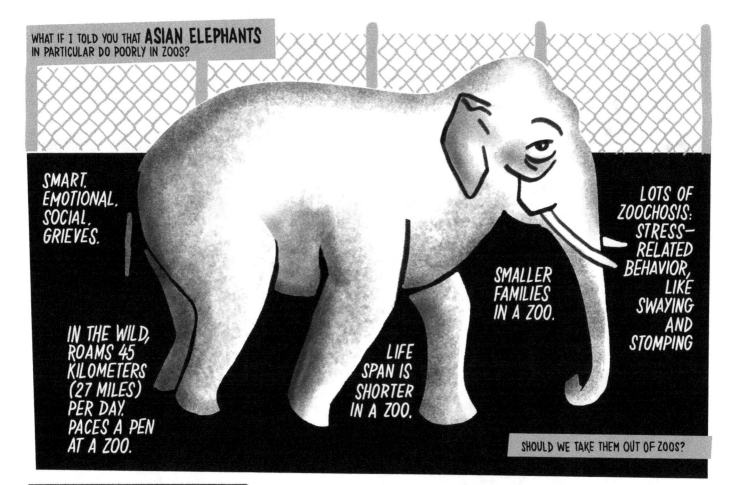

WHAT IF I TOLD YOU THAT **ASIAN ELEPHANTS** IN PARTICULAR DO POORLY IN ZOOS?

SMART. EMOTIONAL. SOCIAL. GRIEVES.

IN THE WILD, ROAMS 45 KILOMETERS (27 MILES) PER DAY. PACES A PEN AT A ZOO.

LIFE SPAN IS SHORTER IN A ZOO.

SMALLER FAMILIES IN A ZOO.

LOTS OF ZOOCHOSIS: STRESS-RELATED BEHAVIOR, LIKE SWAYING AND STOMPING

SHOULD WE TAKE THEM OUT OF ZOOS?

AND IF YOU AGREE THAT MAYBE ONE ANIMAL IS TOO INTELLIGENT OR SENSITIVE TO BE IN A ZOO, WHERE DO YOU STOP?

ZEBRAS ARE CHILL IN CAPTIVITY.

RING-TAILED LEMURS DO WELL JUST ABOUT EVERYWHERE.

BUT THE BIG MONEY IS IN **MISERABLE ANIMALS.**

THE LAST FIFTY YEARS HAVE SEEN **DRAMATIC PROGRESS** IN ZOOS.

ANIMAL ENVIRONMENTS HAVE GONE FROM STERILE CONCRETE TO LAND-LIKE.

On the up side, zoos are always improving.

CARE-TAKING HAS BECOME MORE SOPHISTICATED AND SUCCESSFUL.

PROCUREMENT HAS GONE FROM TRAPPING TO RAISING.

"IT'S HARD FOR ME TO SEE ZOOS AS ANYTHING OTHER THAN BEING ESSENTIAL TO THE LONG-TERM SURVIVAL OF NUMEROUS SPECIES. NOT JUST IN TERMS OF PROTECTING THEM AND BREEDING THEM FOR REINTRODUCTION, BUT TO LEARN ABOUT THEM TO AID THOSE STILL IN THE WILD."

— DR. DAVID HONE, QUEEN MARY, UNIVERSITY OF LONDON

But are humans doing enough for animals?

RIGHT NOW, THERE'S SO MUCH CONCERN FOR GLOBAL WARMING THAT PEOPLE AREN'T HEARING THE WORD ABOUT DISAPPEARING ANIMALS.

ORANGUTAN — ONE OF **2,464** CRITICALLY ENDANGERED ANIMALS

AS DR. WALSH OF CAMBRIDGE UNIVERSITY SAYS: "I FEEL LIKE SHOUTING, 'HEY, GUYS, YOU COULD END CLIMATE CHANGE TOMORROW AND WE'D STILL BE **FACING THE GREATEST EXTINCTION CRISIS WE'VE EVER SEEN.'"**

COULD ZOOS BE BETTER?

SHOULD HUMANS BE DOING MORE TO HELP WILD ANIMALS BOTH IN AND OUT OF CAPTIVITY?

I THINK SO. BUT, YOU KNOW.

I'M A BEAR.

Animals need you!

WANT TO HELP?

SEARCH THE WEB FOR "CHARITY NAVIGATOR ANIMALS." YOU'LL FIND OVER 500 DIFFERENT ANIMAL-RELATED CHARITIES RATED FOR ACCOUNTABILITY AND TRANSPARENCY. ANY AMOUNT HELPS.

ONE OF MY FAVORITE CHARITIES IS THE WILDLIFE CONSERVATION NETWORK AT WILDNET.ORG. YOU CAN LEARN MORE ABOUT THEIR WORK ON THEIR SITE OR AT YOUTUBE.

IF YOU LIKE ZOOS, GO VISIT ONE — OR VOLUNTEER.

THANKS FOR READING!

GHOST SLUG

THE NIGHT HUNTER

BY SALAKJIT

This bizarre-looking creature was first discovered in 2006 in Wales and officially named, *Selenochlamys Ysbryda*, in 2008.

Its scientific name comes from a Latinized form of the Welsh ysbryd (meaning ghost or spirit), referring to its appearance and nocturnal habits.

A pallid body with no eyes,

this creature crawls out at night to hunt.

Earthworms are their feed.

Using its sharp, blade-like teeth,

CRUNCH

CRUNCH

It sucks up its prey like noodles.

Normally around 6.4 cm (2.5 inches) long, when stalking its prey, it can stretch out to 12.7 cm (5 inches) long.

After the bloody hunt, the ghost slug retreats to its subterranean lair.

To wait for the sunset that will bring the terror of... the Ghost Slug.

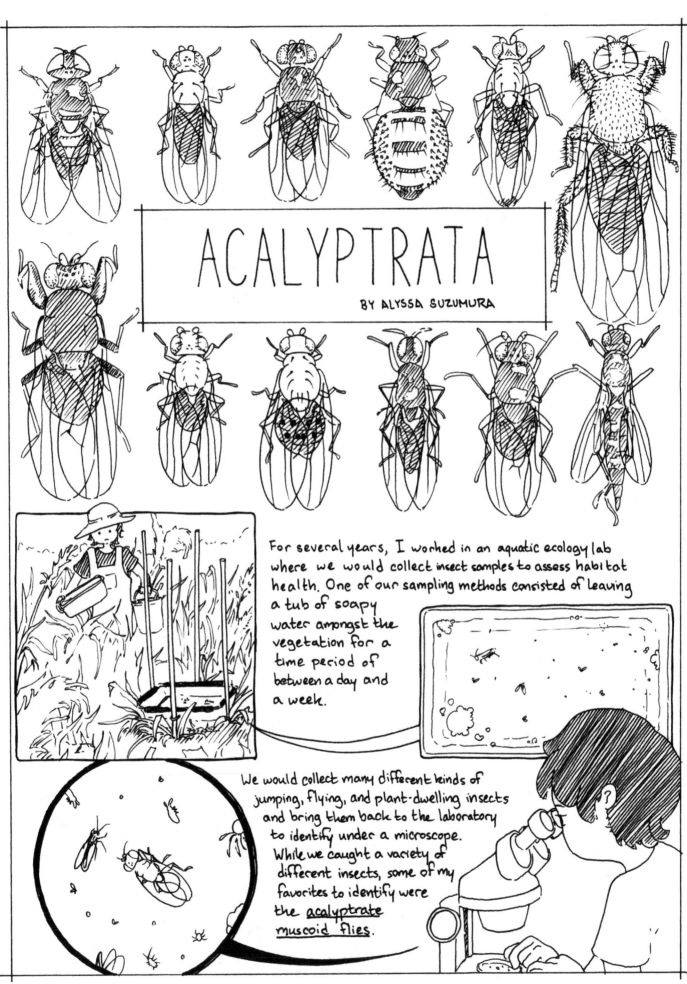

ACALYPTRATA

BY ALYSSA SUZUMURA

For several years, I worked in an aquatic ecology lab where we would collect insect samples to assess habitat health. One of our sampling methods consisted of leaving a tub of soapy water amongst the vegetation for a time period of between a day and a week.

We would collect many different kinds of jumping, flying, and plant-dwelling insects and bring them back to the laboratory to identify under a microscope. While we caught a variety of different insects, some of my favorites to identify were the <u>acalyptrate muscoid flies</u>.

True flies or "diptera" can be differentiated from similar-looking flying insects by having only one pair of wings, but the diptera is a very large group containing a diversity of morphologically different groups. Members of all groups were easily collected in our traps but using the following features, the acalyptrates can easily be separated from the others:

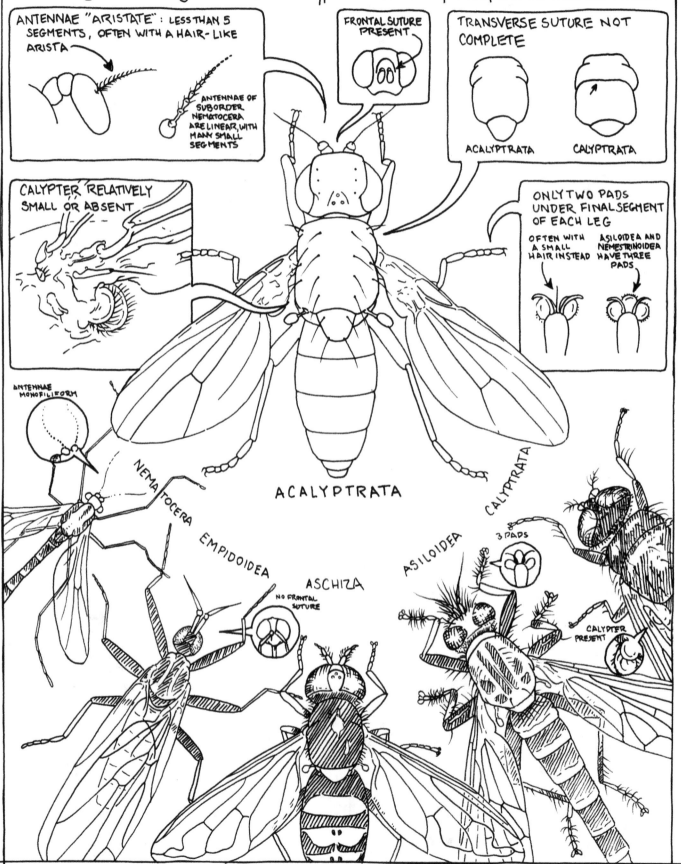

Most acalyptrates are just considered "fruit flies" by the layperson but it's actually a diverse group containing over 60 families of which only 2 are actually "fruit flies".

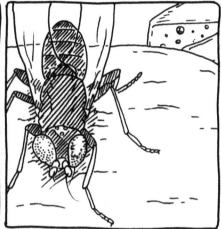

This isn't surprising considering that most of these flies are very small.

Additionally, many of these flies live in highly specific habitats that are hidden from the casual observer.

Haleomyia petrolei larvae live in pools of petroleum.

Some species of Strongylophthalmyids live in the narrow spaces under tree bark.

...2 rows of acrostichal bristles, 3 pairs of postsuturals, prescutellars present...

Interested in looking closer yet?

Despite the flies' diminutive size, entomologists can identify different species based on a combination of anatomical characteristics.

Dipterists (those who study flies) spend a lot of time looking at patterns of setae (bug hairs) and patterns of wing veins.

The Manual of Nearctic Diptera is the most comprehensive identification guide for North American flies.

THE HEAD

We'll start with the head since it's the part at the front of the fly.

POSTOCELLAR BRISTLES
Do these bristles lean towards, away, or parallel to each other?

WHAT ACTUALLY IS A "BRISTLE"?
Bristles are stiff hairs that generally stand away from the body.

"spurs" and "spikes" are extensions of the exoskeleton

Regular hairs are softer, thinner, and more bendable.

In addition to patterns of setae mentioned before, locations of hairs, antennae size and shape, presence or absence of ocelli (simple eyes), texture, color, and shape the common

are some of features you will find in identification guides.

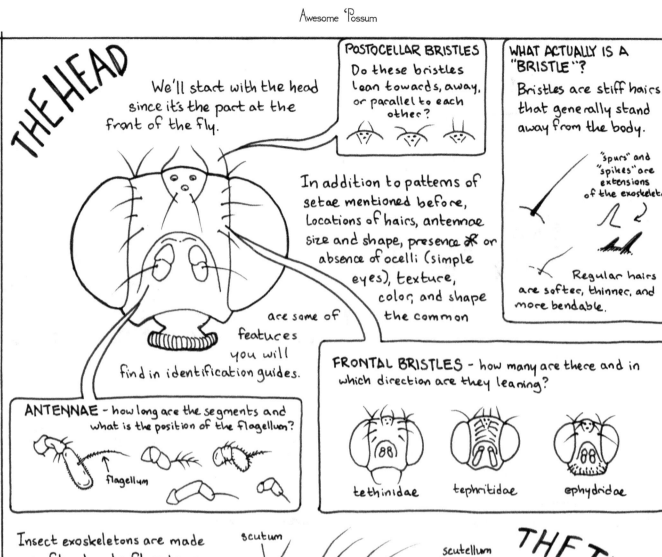

ANTENNAE - how long are the segments and what is the position of the flagellum?

flagellum

FRONTAL BRISTLES - how many are there and in which direction are they leaning?

tethinidae   tephritidae   ephydridae

Insect exoskeletons are made up of hard and soft sections of chitin, and all of these sections have their own names (some even have multiple names).

THE THORAX

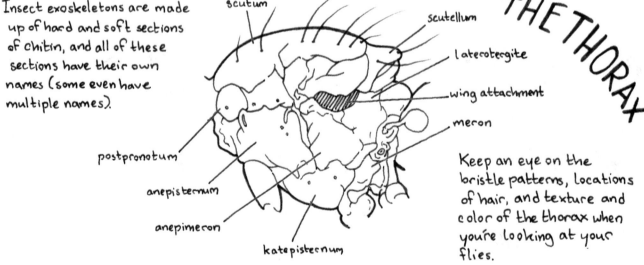

scutum
scutellum
laterotergite
wing attachment
meron
postpronotum
anepisternum
anepimeron
katepisternum

Keep an eye on the bristle patterns, locations of hair, and texture and color of the thorax when you're looking at your flies.

Can you see the differences in the patterns of bristles?

All of these flies are in the same family, but these species all look pretty different...

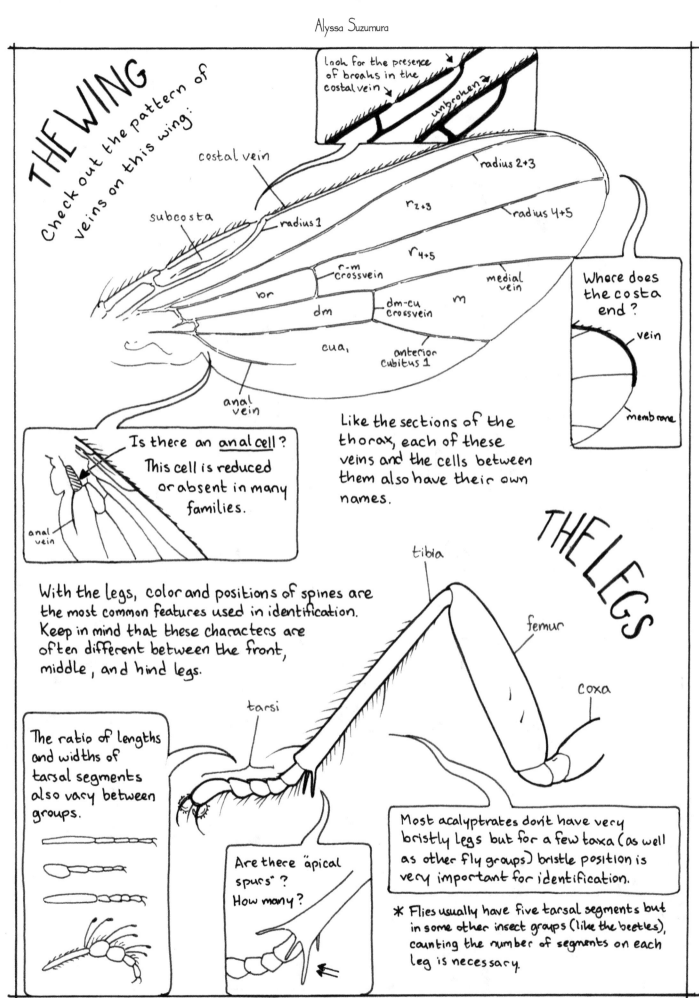

THE WING

Check out the pattern of veins on this wing:

Look for the presence of breaks in the costal vein

unbroken?

costal vein

subcosta

radius 1

radius 2+3

r_{2+3}

radius 4+5

r_{4+5}

r-m crossvein

br

dm

dm-cu crossvein

medial vein

m

cua_1

anterior cubitus 1

anal vein

Where does the costa end?

vein

membrane

Is there an <u>anal cell</u>? This cell is reduced or absent in many families.

anal vein

Like the sections of the thorax, each of these veins and the cells between them also have their own names.

THE LEGS

tibia

femur

coxa

With the legs, color and positions of spines are the most common features used in identification. Keep in mind that these characters are often different between the front, middle, and hind legs.

tarsi

The ratio of lengths and widths of tarsal segments also vary between groups.

Are there "apical spurs"? How many?

Most acalyptrates don't have very bristly legs but for a few taxa (as well as other fly groups) bristle position is very important for identification.

* Flies usually have five tarsal segments but in some other insect groups (like the beetles), counting the number of segments on each leg is necessary.

THE ABDOMEN

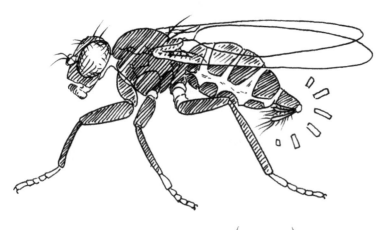

Characters on the abdomen, such as bristles, color, and shape are sometimes used but the more important detail is the insect's genitalia, which is often needed to identify to the species level, especially in groups with many similar-looking species.

These three genitalia are from male flies of the same genus of shore flies, *Allotrichoma*. While these three species are closely related, their genitalia are distinctly different in shape and hair patterns.

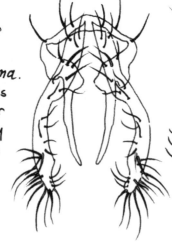

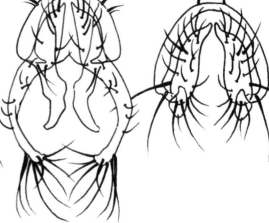

A. dynatum   A. lacteum   A. atrilabre

Even though these flies aren't flashy or charismatic, I like them because despite the disinterest of humans, they are living complex and diverse lives all around us.

THE GHOST OWL

AKA BARN OWL
AKA TYTO ALBA

BY BERNARDO O. DIAS

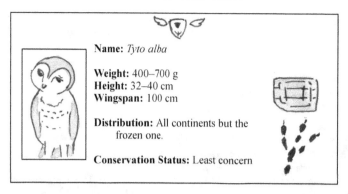

Name: *Tyto alba*

Weight: 400–700 g
Height: 32–40 cm
Wingspan: 100 cm

Distribution: All continents but the frozen one.

Conservation Status: Least concern

TOWER OWL, STONE OWL, BARN OWL. T. ALBA OFTEN NESTS IN MAN-MADE PLACES, AS THE NAMES SUGGEST.
THEY ALSO LIKE HOLLOW TREES.

DON'T BE SURPRISED IF YOU SEE A WHITE SHAPE FLYING OFF AN OLD BUILDING.

T. ALBA ADAPTS TO WHATEVER PREY IS MORE COMMON IN ITS TERRITORY. EVEN THEN, ABOUT 90% CONSISTS OF SMALL MAMMALS SUCH AS MICE.

A FIELD WITH GHOST OWLS IS A FIELD WITH FEW PESTS.

BIG EYES HELP THEM SEE IN THE DARK

THE HEART SHAPE OF THE FACE WORKS LIKE PARABOLIC ANTENNAE ALLOWING OWLS TO HEAR BETTER.

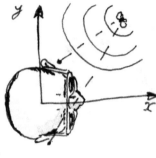

BECAUSE OUR EARS ARE ON DIFFERENT PARTS OF OUR HEAD, SOUNDS DO NOT REACH THEM EQUALLY.

OUR BRAIN USES THAT DIFFERENCE TO JUDGE WHERE THE SOUND COMES FROM.

OWLS HAVE AN EXTRA TRICK. THE EAR CANALS HAVE DIFFERENT HEIGHTS.

THIS GIVES THEM AN EDGE IN FIGURING OUT THE HEIGHT OF THE SOURCE OF SOUND.

TRY IT OUT:
COVER YOUR EYES AND HAVE SOMEONE YOU TRUST SNAP THEIR FINGERS NEARBY.

CAN YOU POINT TO THEIR POSITION? AND CAN YOU TELL WHEN THEY ARE HIGHER OR LOWER?

T. ALBA CAN LISTEN TO THE PREY'S POSITION, BE IT LEFT, RIGHT, UP, OR DOWN. THEY CAN CATCH PREY IN NEAR COMPLETE DARKNESS.

THEIR WINGS ARE PRETTY BIG — ABOUT A METER TIP TO TIP.

IT HELPS THEM TO STAY ALOFT IN LOW, SLOW FLIGHTS AND TO KEEP THE WING FLAPPING TO A MINIMUM FOR SILENCE.

THE WINGS HAVE OTHER TRICKS TO MAKE THEM MORE SILENT SO THEY CAN SNEAK UP ON THEIR PREY.

FOR EXAMPLE, SMALL "SERRATIONS" IN THE FEATHERS SEEM TO CHANGE THE AIR-FLOW AND REDUCE NOISE IN FLIGHT.

WE'RE STILL TRYING TO FIGURE OUT ALL THE SECRETS.

THE GHOST OWL: ENHANCED SENSES, SILENT, DEADLY STRIKES.

THEY ARE FEATHERY, FLYING NINJAS.

THE END

Ä'ày Chù (Slim's River.)

by Rachel Ford

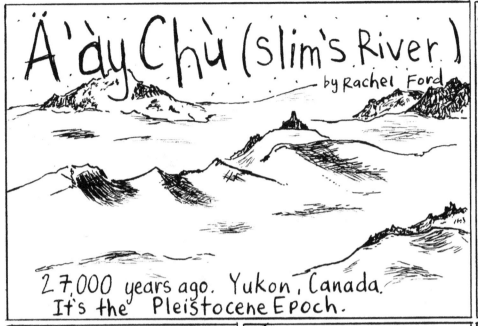

27,000 years ago. Yukon, Canada. It's the Pleistocene Epoch.

Half of North America is covered in a huge glacier.

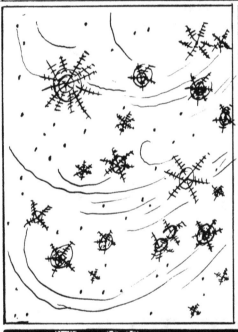

Snow piles on snow...

layers on layers.

Snow in lower layers are under intense pressure.

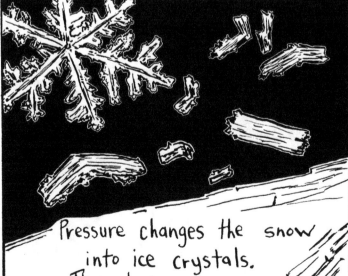

Pressure changes the snow into ice crystals. The glacier grows.

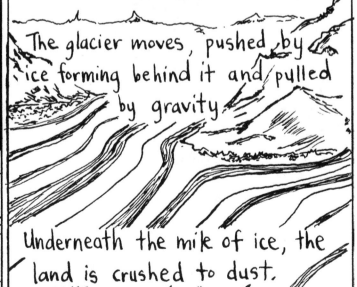

The glacier moves, pushed by ice forming behind it and pulled by gravity.

Underneath the mile of ice, the land is crushed to dust.

14,000 years ago. It's the beginning of the Holocene Epoch.

The North begins to melt.

Surface water runs over the ice...

into deep holes that bore through the glacier.

Sometimes all the way to the land below.

Glaciers retreat when more ice melts in the summer than is replaced in the winter.

The water and exposed land allow pioneer plants to grow.

A few thousand years ago. A river flows from the toe of the retreating glacier.

The land fills with plants.

Poplar and willow grow first.

A forest of white spruce follows.

The plants bring animals.

grizzly bear

collared pika

Mountain goat

Dall sheep

black bear

Ice age megafauna like woolly mammoth, giant beaver, giant short-faced bear, Yukon horse, and Beringian lion have already gone extinct.

The first humans to walk in the valley were the Southern Tutchone people.

They have hunted and fished in the area since the end of the ice age.

Overlooking the glacier is a mountain they name **Ä'ày Dhäl***

*By Itself Mountain

It inspires the name of the river.

Ä'ày Chù*

*By Itself Water

1903 – A gold rush brings prospectors to Ä'ày Chù.

A prospector's horse gets stuck in the river's mud and drowns.

Slim

The mourning prospector names the river after his horse.

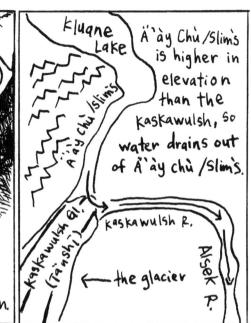

May 2016. The glacier has been feeding two rivers separated by a wall of ice. Over four days, that wall melts and a channel forms between them.

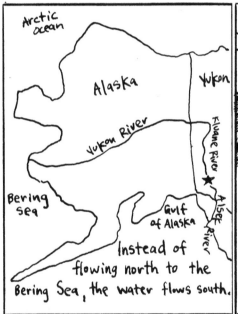

Instead of flowing north to the Bering Sea, the water flows south.

July 2016. Ä'äy Chù / Slim's River is almost completely dry. The wind kicks up dust created by the glacier over millennia.

. Snow to Ice

to Water

to Life

to Dust.

END.

Ross Wood Studlar

CHICKEN SCRATCH

By Elise Smorczewski

Even though we share the Earth with about 20 billion chickens, most people don't think about them except as food. I'm out to change some minds about these actually pretty interesting birds!

Domestic chickens are descended from junglefowl of southeast Asia, of which there are four species:

Green
Gallus varius

Red
G. gallus

Grey
G. sonneratii

Ceylon
G. lafayettii

Domestication probably took place in the Indus Valley. The first chickens were kept for fighting, not food.

Egyptians built large ovens to artificially incubate chicken eggs.

750 BCE

Chickens may have been brought to South America by Polynesians before Columbus's travels.

YES!
NO.

Romans used chickens to divine the future and also to eat.

5000 BCE

1350 CE

Orpington
1874 CE
English Class
Buff, Black, Blue, White

American Poultry Association published a guide to chicken breeds, the "Standard of Perfection."

1989 CE

Chicken embryos traveled into space aboard space shuttle Discovery.

2004 CE

Scientists mapped the chickens genome.

Like most birds, only one of a chicken's two ovaries is functional.

A hen can lay one egg every 25 hours.

300

As many as 300 eggs a year.

THE AMAZING EGG!

Yolk
Feeds the embryo

Shell
Protects the contents of the egg

Chalazae
Holds the yolk and embryo centered

Cuticle (Bloom)
Protective coating that helps keep bacteria out

Germinal Disc
Forms the embryo if the egg is fertile

Albumen (Egg White)
Provides moisture and cushion for the embryo

Fertile   Infertile

Air Cell
Pocket of air that allows the embryo to breathe

All of the eggs for sale at the grocery store are infertile. A hen can lay eggs without a rooster.

How Old Is This Egg?
You can check the age of an egg by putting it in water. This is because the air cell grows over time. Use the egg after testing because water damages the bloom.

FRESH   1 WEEK   3 WEEKS   NO GOOD

The Jersey Giant hen can weigh up to 5 kilograms and can lay eggs weighing over 70 grams. Serama bantams are tiny chickens weighing only 500 grams or less and lay tiny eggs weighing under 24 grams.

A "Large" grocery store egg is around 57 grams.

Jumbo! 70g+

Large! 57g

pee wee! 24g

SOAP

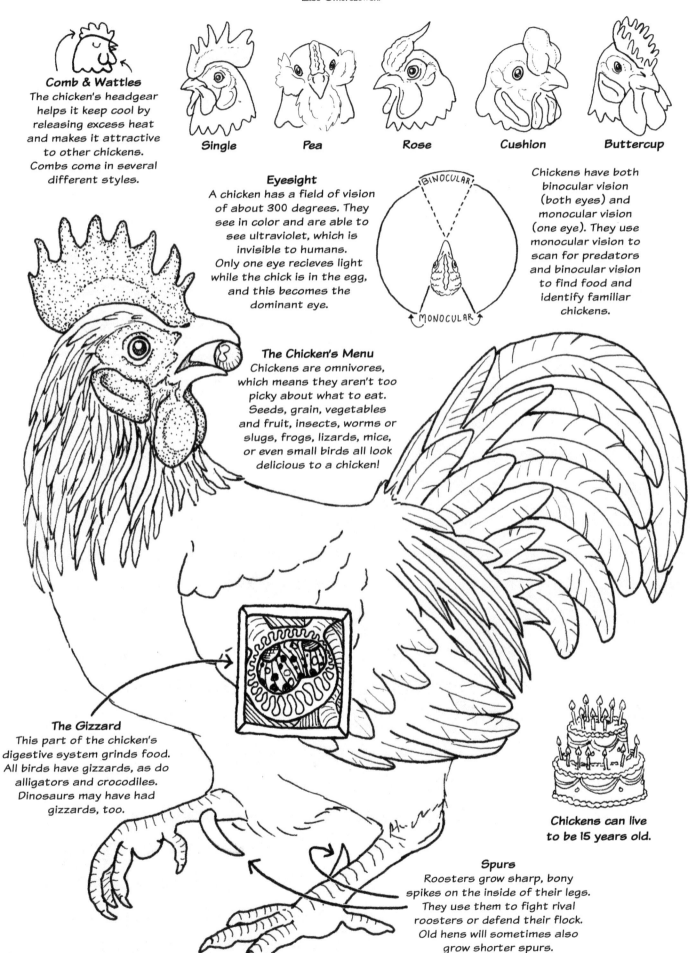

Elise Smorczewski

Comb & Wattles
The chicken's headgear helps it keep cool by releasing excess heat and makes it attractive to other chickens. Combs come in several different styles.

Single

Pea

Rose

Cushion

Buttercup

Eyesight
A chicken has a field of vision of about 300 degrees. They see in color and are able to see ultraviolet, which is invisible to humans. Only one eye recieves light while the chick is in the egg, and this becomes the dominant eye.

BINOCULAR

MONOCULAR

Chickens have both binocular vision (both eyes) and monocular vision (one eye). They use monocular vision to scan for predators and binocular vision to find food and identify familiar chickens.

The Chicken's Menu
Chickens are omnivores, which means they aren't too picky about what to eat. Seeds, grain, vegetables and fruit, insects, worms or slugs, frogs, lizards, mice, or even small birds all look delicious to a chicken!

The Gizzard
This part of the chicken's digestive system grinds food. All birds have gizzards, as do alligators and crocodiles. Dinosaurs may have had gizzards, too.

Chickens can live to be 15 years old.

Spurs
Roosters grow sharp, bony spikes on the inside of their legs. They use them to fight rival roosters or defend their flock. Old hens will sometimes also grow shorter spurs.

FANTASTIC FEATHERS

Short and broad wings

Can Chickens Fly?
Yes, but not very well. Chickens will often fly up onto a perch to roost for the night, and can fly short distances to evade predators. However, like their junglefowl ancestors, they are adapted to life on the ground.

Silkie Feather

Silkies
This chicken breed has a certain feather mutation that causes the feathers to be soft with a furlike texture.

Naked Neck
Also called "Turkens" they look like a chicken-turkey cross. This breed has a mutatution that causes parts of the body to be featherless.

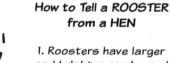

Frizzle Feather

Frizzle
This breed's feather mutation causes the chicken's feathers to curve up and away from the body instead of towards it. This causes an interesting ruffled texture.

How to Tell a ROOSTER from a HEN

1. Roosters have larger and brighter combs and wattles.

2. Only roosters crow.

3. The feathers of the neck, back and tail will be pointed on a rooster, and rounded on a hen.

A rooster may also have two tall curved tail feathers, called "sickle feathers."

4. Roosters have spurs, and hens usually do not.

Chickens make between 25 and 30 different noises. They are able to communicate feelings to the rest of their flock, such as contentment, dominance, distress, and frustration.

CHICKEN TALK

Peep, peep?

Peep-peep!

Chicks peep to each other in the three days before hatching. This encourages chicks that are developing slower to hurry up so they all hatch at the same time.

buh buh buh BAGAK

Alarm Calls

If a member of the flock notices a predator, they will make a loud noise to alert the other chickens. They use calls unique to each type of predator, so if a rooster makes a hawk alarm call, hens will look for shelter to hide underneath.

Come Eat!

When a rooster finds something to eat, he will call out to his hens while mimicking eating. Mother hens make this same call to their chicks.

BUK BUK BUK
BUK-BUK
BUK

Are Chickens Smart?

Probably smarter than most people give them credit for! Here's seven facts that might have you rethinking the term bird brain.

Even as young chicks, chickens can do basic math such as addition and subtraction.

Chickens can understand the passage of time and will wait for larger rewards.

Chickens show empathy for other flock members in distress.

Chickens can be trained to do tricks and run agility courses.

They can recognize up to 100 other chickens and also remember human individuals.

They have great memories and can remember sequences of events or locations of food.

Chickens are able to use deductive reasoning to use what they know to learn new information.

CHICKEN  NATIONS

Chickens have been kept all across the world for hundreds of years. Along the way, they have picked up regional differences that have now become established as over 350 chicken breeds. Here are some of my favorite breeds with the countries credited with their creation.

Australorp	Bearded d'Uccle	Araucana	Cochin
Australia	Belgium	Chile	China
Fayoumi	Faverolles	Lakenvelder	Aseel
Egypt	France	Germany	India
Leghorn	Onagadori	Brabanter	Minorca
Italy	Japan	Netherlands	Spain
Orloff	Sultan	Modern Game	Rhode Island Red
Russia	Turkey	United Kingdom	United States

Taking a Peek at the One-Eyed Sphinx Moth

Smerinthus cerisyi

by Anita K. Boyle

This summer, on my way to the Poetry Shed, I noticed what looked like a few leaves stuck to the steps. But I was wrong—

On closer inspection, the leaves were actually a couple of moths mating.

"How romantic," I thought.

So I crammed them into a Mason jar, and brought them into my studio.

The next day, I found small, bright green eggs all over the jar, singly and in groups, especially at the bottom, but on the sides, too.

I scrubbed a ten-gallon fish tank sparkling clean, then added some dirt.

1½ inches of clean dirt

A willow tree grows beside the Poetry Shed, so I cut a few leafy twigs, and put them inside for the moths to climb on.

Mesh Top

Finally, I put moths, eggs and Mason jar into their new home.

Sadly, but predictably, the male moth died the next day. The female one-eyed sphinx moth continued to lay eggs for a few more days before she, too, passed on to the great light bulb in the sky.

But she left behind close to 200 eggs.

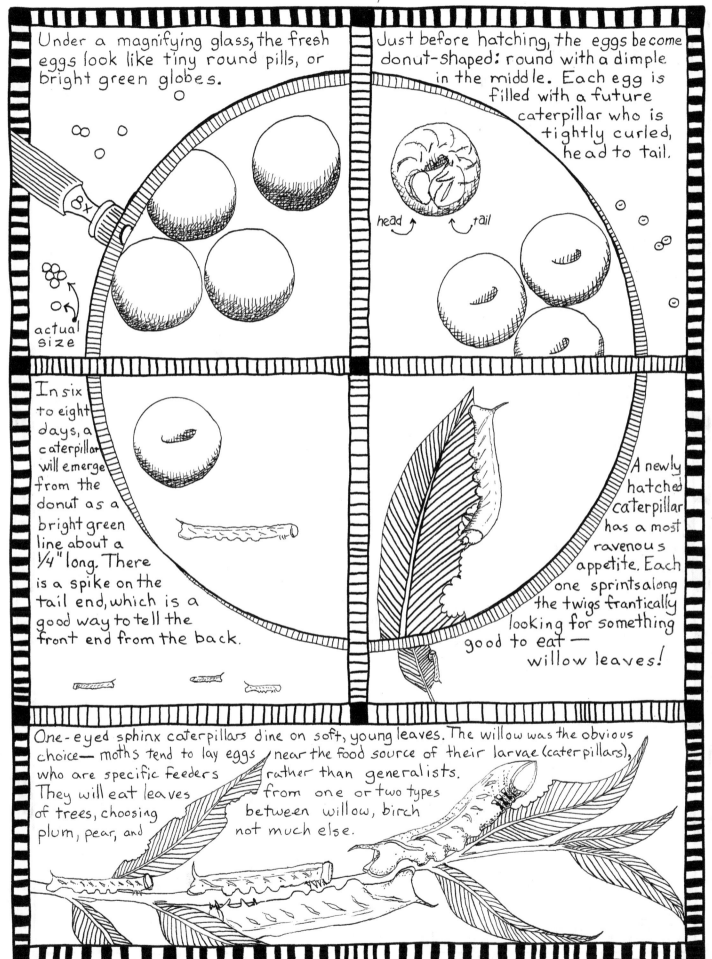

Under a magnifying glass, the fresh eggs look like tiny round pills, or bright green globes.

8x

actual size

Just before hatching, the eggs become donut-shaped: round with a dimple in the middle. Each egg is filled with a future caterpillar who is tightly curled, head to tail.

head ↑   ↑ tail

In six to eight days, a caterpillar will emerge from the donut as a bright green line about a 1/4" long. There is a spike on the tail end, which is a good way to tell the front end from the back.

A newly hatched caterpillar has a most ravenous appetite. Each one sprints along the twigs frantically looking for something good to eat — willow leaves!

One-eyed sphinx caterpillars dine on soft, young leaves. The willow was the obvious choice— moths tend to lay eggs near the food source of their larvae (caterpillars), who are specific feeders rather than generalists. They will eat leaves from one or two types of trees, choosing between willow, birch plum, pear, and not much else.

The Fantastic Anatomy of a One-Eyed Sphinx Caterpillar

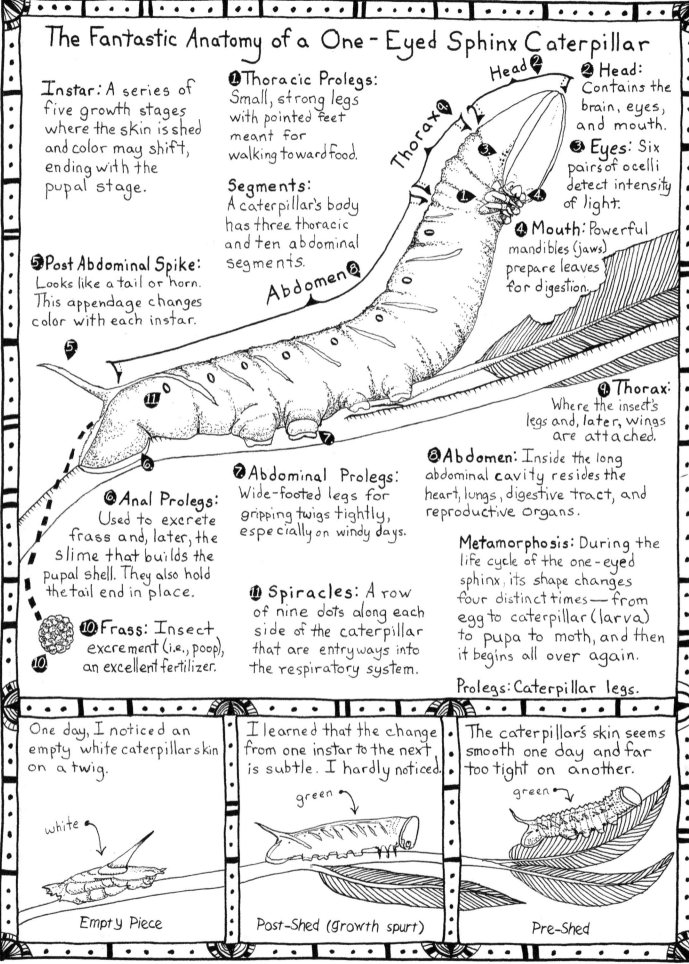

Instar: A series of five growth stages where the skin is shed and color may shift, ending with the pupal stage.

❶Thoracic Prolegs: Small, strong legs with pointed feet meant for walking toward food.

Segments: A caterpillar's body has three thoracic and ten abdominal segments.

Head ❷

Thorax ❾

❷ **Head:** Contains the brain, eyes, and mouth.

❸ **Eyes:** Six pairs of ocelli detect intensity of light.

❹ **Mouth:** Powerful mandibles (jaws) prepare leaves for digestion.

❺Post Abdominal Spike: Looks like a tail or horn. This appendage changes color with each instar.

Abdomen ❽

❾ **Thorax:** Where the insect's legs and, later, wings are attached.

❻Anal Prolegs: Used to excrete frass and, later, the slime that builds the pupal shell. They also hold the tail end in place.

❼Abdominal Prolegs: Wide-footed legs for gripping twigs tightly, especially on windy days.

❽ **Abdomen:** Inside the long abdominal cavity resides the heart, lungs, digestive tract, and reproductive organs.

Metamorphosis: During the life cycle of the one-eyed sphinx, its shape changes four distinct times—from egg to caterpillar (larva) to pupa to moth, and then it begins all over again.

❿Frass: Insect excrement (i.e., poop), an excellent fertilizer.

⓫ Spiracles: A row of nine dots along each side of the caterpillar that are entryways into the respiratory system.

Prolegs: Caterpillar legs.

One day, I noticed an empty white caterpillar skin on a twig.

white

Empty Piece

I learned that the change from one instar to the next is subtle. I hardly noticed.

green

Post-Shed (growth spurt)

The caterpillar's skin seems smooth one day and far too tight on another.

green

Pre-Shed

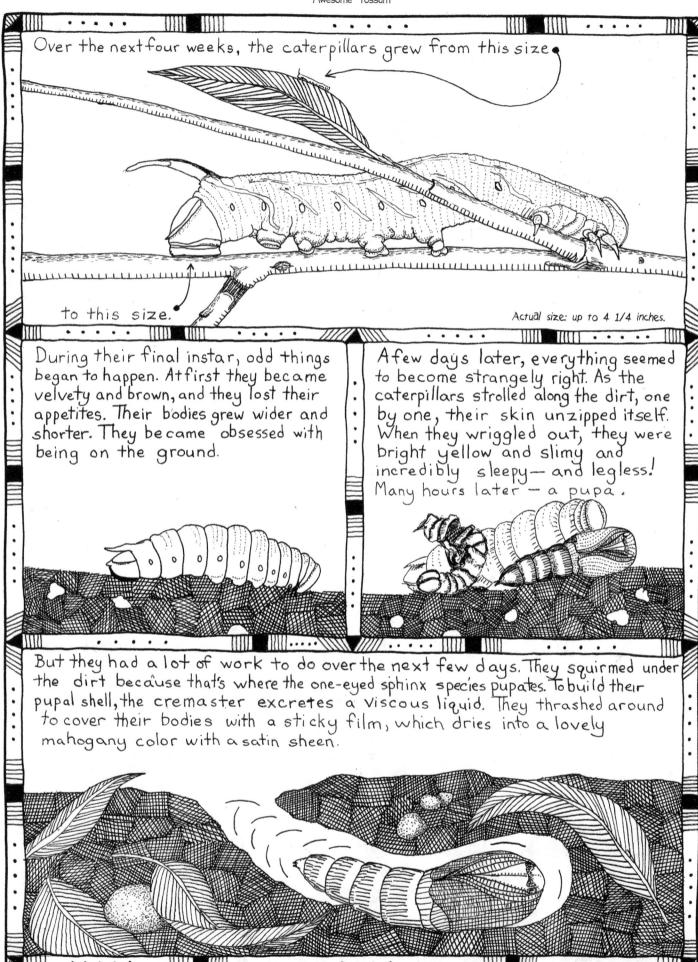

Over the next four weeks, the caterpillars grew from this size.

to this size.

Actual size: up to 4 1/4 inches.

During their final instar, odd things began to happen. At first they became velvety and brown, and they lost their appetites. Their bodies grew wider and shorter. They became obsessed with being on the ground.

A few days later, everything seemed to become strangely right. As the caterpillars strolled along the dirt, one by one, their skin unzipped itself. When they wriggled out, they were bright yellow and slimy and incredibly sleepy— and legless! Many hours later — a pupa.

But they had a lot of work to do over the next few days. They squirmed under the dirt because that's where the one-eyed sphinx species pupates. To build their pupal shell, the cremaster excretes a viscous liquid. They thrashed around to cover their bodies with a sticky film, which dries into a lovely mahogany color with a satin sheen.

The Marvelous Sections of a One-Eyed Sphinx Pupa

Pupa: Preparatory stage from which the moth will emerge.

❶Abdominal Segments: These five segments contain all vital organs, except the brain.

❷Antenna: The source of the moth's olfactory radar for navigation and balance during flight.

❸Head: A small bump atop the pupa which carries the brain and eyes.

❹Mesothoracic Leg: The middle leg of the three pairs insects have.

Abdominal Segments ❶

❺Cremaster: Emits the slimy liquid that spreads over the pupa to create the shell.

❻Metathoracic Leg: The hind leg, which is difficult to see on a pupa.

❼Prothorax: The front "face" portion of the thorax, which accommodates both legs and wings.

❽Forewing: This appendage looks like the headdress of the Egyptian Sphinx. This wing will cover the lower wing, which has an eye-like spot on it. Hence the name one-eyed sphinx moth.

❾Prothoracic Leg: The future front leg of the moth.

Mouth: The pupa gives the moth only a vestigal mouth since the moth doesn't eat anything at all.

All winter long, the pupae will be at rest underground. They wait for the temperature to warm, the hours of sunlight to lengthen, and the humidity to become just right. The wait will be long and cold, and they will need great patience to hold still as death in the dark leafy humus until their metamorphosis finishes with an eclosion — the act of emergance as a moth.

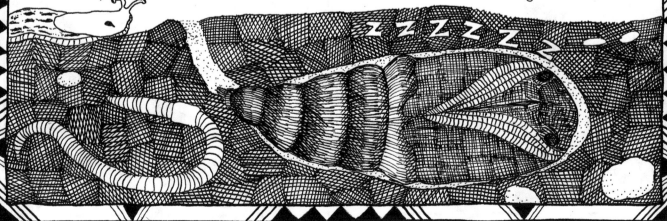

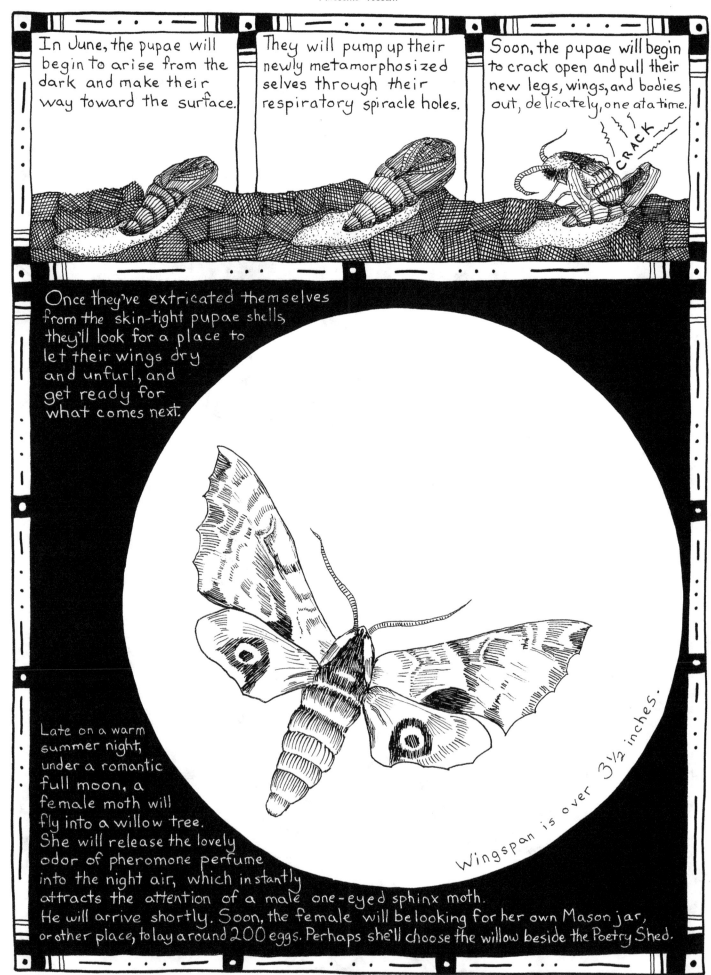

In June, the pupae will begin to arise from the dark and make their way toward the surface.

They will pump up their newly metamorphosized selves through their respiratory spiracle holes.

Soon, the pupae will begin to crack open and pull their new legs, wings, and bodies out, delicately, one at a time.

CRACK

Once they've extricated themselves from the skin-tight pupae shells, they'll look for a place to let their wings dry and unfurl, and get ready for what comes next.

Late on a warm summer night, under a romantic full moon, a female moth will fly into a willow tree. She will release the lovely odor of pheromone perfume into the night air, which instantly attracts the attention of a male one-eyed sphinx moth.
He will arrive shortly. Soon, the female will be looking for her own Mason jar, or other place, to lay around 200 eggs. Perhaps she'll choose the willow beside the Poetry Shed.

Wingspan is over 3½ inches.

We all live & we all die & we all have bones inside. ~n.l.canyon

BONE
Collector

By Nancy Canyon

I've picked up bones on walks along country roads, on hikes in the woods, and while beach combing.

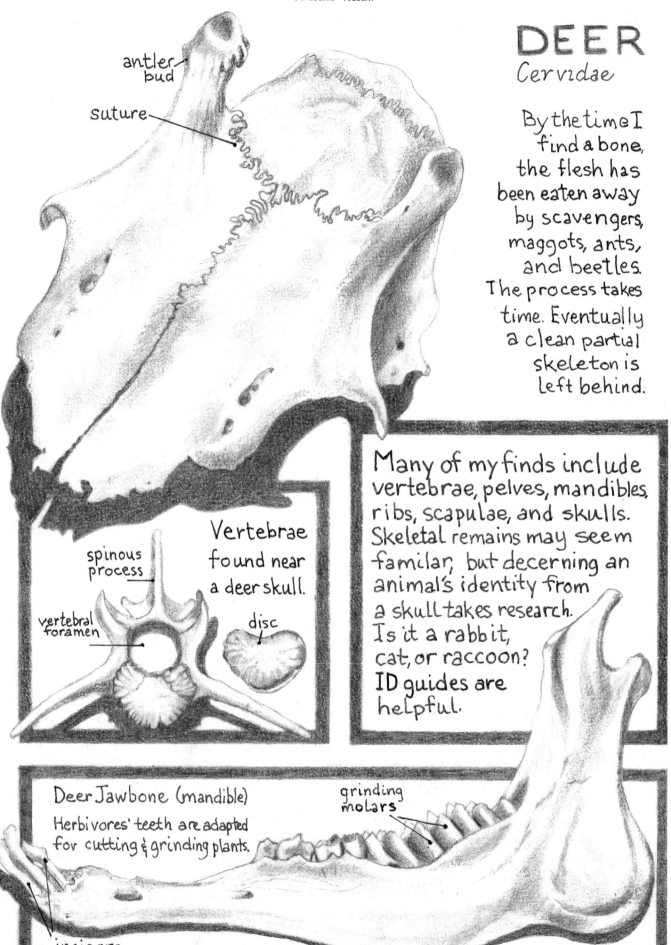

antler bud

suture

DEER
Cervidae

By the time I find a bone, the flesh has been eaten away by scavengers, maggots, ants, and beetles. The process takes time. Eventually a clean partial skeleton is left behind.

Many of my finds include vertebrae, pelves, mandibles, ribs, scapulae, and skulls. Skeletal remains may seem familar, but decerning an animal's identity from a skull takes research. Is it a rabbit, cat, or raccoon? ID guides are helpful.

Vertebrae found near a deer skull.

spinous process

vertebral foramen

disc

Deer Jawbone (mandible)

Herbivores' teeth are adapted for cutting & grinding plants.

grinding molars

incisors

RACCOON
Procyonidae

The bones I collect are from animals who have been dead a long time. Some **had** good lives. The raccoon family that nested in the bigleaf maple out front of a home where I once lived was always raiding the compost bin. The largest one was very old, with one blind eye and a noticeable limp.

There are people who feel weird about touching something that used to be alive. The yellowed bones I find aren't dirty; however, some collectors wear gloves.

Raccoon pelvis

Raccoon nest

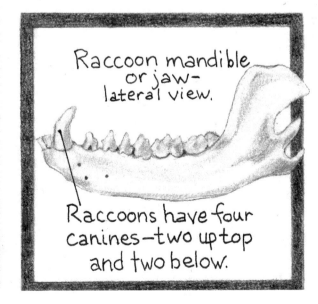

Raccoon mandible or jaw-lateral view.

Raccoons have four canines—two up top and two below.

DOMESTIC DOG
Canis lupus familiaris

A dog skull has eye sockets facing forward indicating a predator. It's canines, also called fangs, are meant for tearing meat.

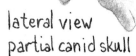

lateral view
partial canid skull

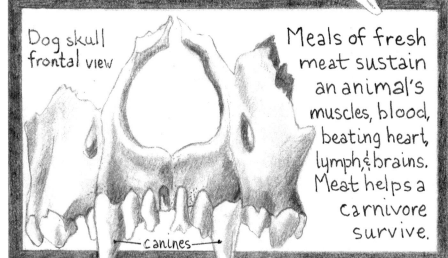

Dog skull frontal view

—canines—

Meals of fresh meat sustain an animal's muscles, blood, beating heart, lymph, & brains. Meat helps a carnivore survive.

"Eyes in front, likes to hunt; eyes at side, likes to hide."

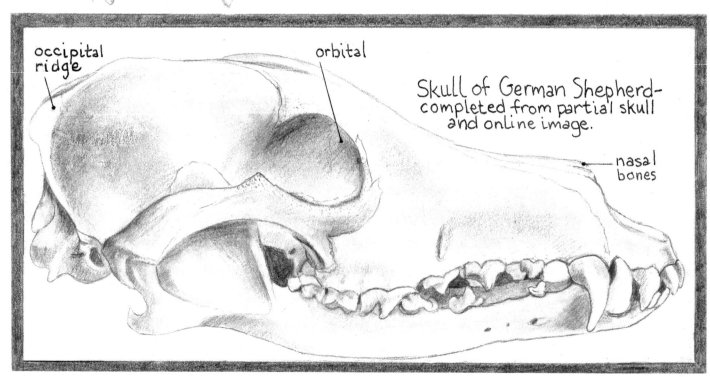

occipital ridge

orbital

Skull of German Shepherd- completed from partial skull and online image.

nasal bones

HOUSE CAT
Felis catus

Cats have strong canine teeth meant for gripping, tearing, and chewing meat.

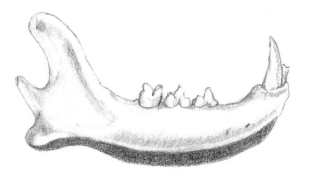

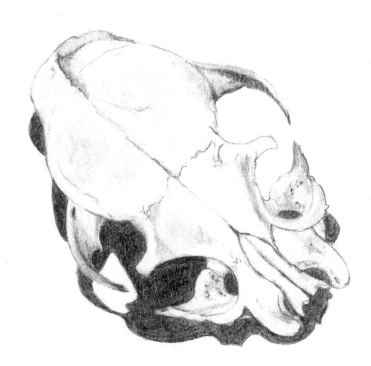

Bones of the skull

temporal
parietal
lacrimal
frontal
orbital

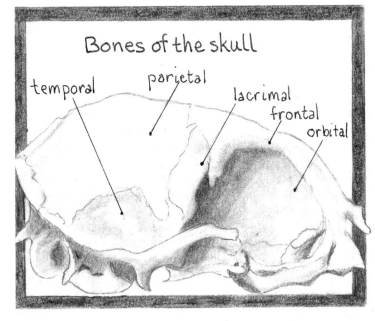

Skull of domestic cat, ventral view

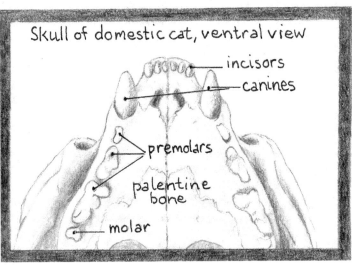

incisors
canines
premolars
palentine bone
molar

Because I practice craniosacral therapy, a modality that gently moves the plates of the cranium in both humans and animals, I like observing cranial landmarks: sutures, ridges, and bone shapes that make up skulls. I know how to feel orbital, occipital, frontal, parietal, and temporal bones. My cat's tolerance for my searching fingers doesn't give me much time to feel the layout of his cranial bones. His large round orbitals facing forward are obvious, as are his mandible and maxilla bones. Examining his canines and incisors can be dangerous, to say the least. My found cat's skull allows me to observe the cranial plates physically and safely.

RABBIT
Leporidae

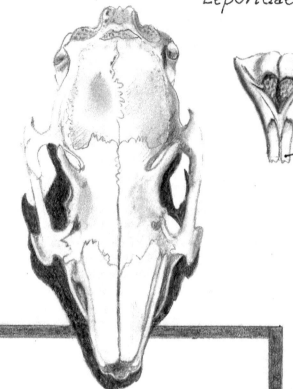

incisors

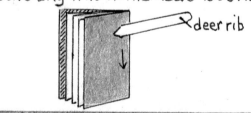

"extra" incisors

When I see a rabbit skull with eye sockets on the sides, I recall the rabbits that run across the path, diving into the brush as my leashed dog goes crazy, trying to catch the little critters. Bigger, faster animals kill many smaller animals because they need lots of fuel to animate strong muscular bodies.

Rabbit mandible

Some bones make it into my art or become tools. A deer rib, after rasping and polishing, was turned into a bone folder to crease paper for stitching into homemade books.

deer rib

Bone-collecting Equipment
(bucket)   (gloves)   (spade)

If you want to become a bone collector like me, keep an eye out when you walk along rural roads, in the woods, or on the beach.

The Woman Without Fear

BY SPRATTY LIN

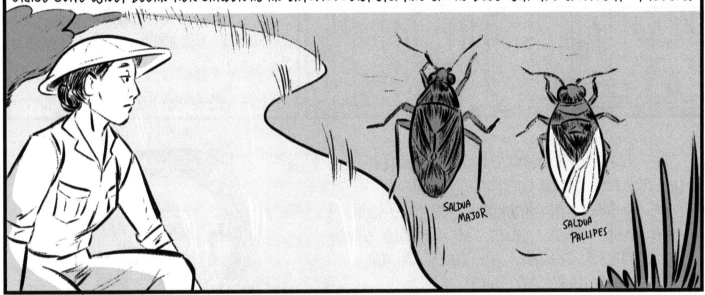

GRACE OLIVE WILEY BEGAN HER CAREER AS AN ENTOMOLOGIST STUDYING SHORE BUGS WITH THE UNIVERSITY OF KANSAS.

SALDUA MAJOR

SALDUA PALLIPES

SHE BEGAN STUDYING RATTLESNAKES IN HER MID-30'S WHILE DOING FIELDWORK IN THE SOUTHWESTERN UNITED STATES, WHICH WOULD SPARK A LIFE-LONG PASSION FOR REPTILES.

WITHIN A FEW YEARS, WILEY BECAME THE FIRST PERSON TO SUCESSFULLY BREED RATTLESNAKES IN CAPTIVITY.

IN 1923 WILEY WAS NAMED A CURATOR AT THE MINNEAPOLIS PUBLIC LIBRARY'S NATURAL HISTORY MUSEUM.

INITIALLY SHE GARNERED A LOT OF ATTENTION FOR BEING A FEMALE CURATOR OF REPTILES, WHICH WAS HIGHLY UNUSUAL AT THE TIME.

THE FEAR OF SNAKES IS CULTIVATED. WE ARE NOT BORN WITH IT. CHILDREN LOVE SNAKES AS NATURALLY AS THEY LOVE CATS AND DOGS. DON'T BE AFRAID OF A REPTILE'S TONGUE. THE ONLY ANIMAL THAT CAN HURT YOU WITH IT'S TONGUE IS A DEMON.

EVEN A VENOMOUS SNAKE IS HARMLESS IF PROPERLY TRAINED.

EVENTUALLY SHE BECAME FAMOUS FOR HER CONTROVERSIAL OPINIONS AND DANGEROUS HANDLING TECHNIQUES. SHE TOOK ADVANTAGE OF HER SPOTLIGHT, SEEKING TO CHANGE THE PUBLIC'S NEGATIVE OPINIONS ABOUT SNAKES.

WILEY'S METHOD OF HABITUATING SNAKES TO HANDLING INVOLVED FIRST TOUCHING THEM WITH A PADDED STICK,

LEAVING ARTICLES OF HER CLOTHING IN THEIR ENCLOSURES SO THEY WOULD RECOGNIZE HER SMELL AS NON-THREATENING,

AND FINALLY, GENTLY TOUCHING AND HOLDING THEM FOR INCREASING AMOUNTS OF TIME.

SHE REFUSED TO USE CONVENTIONAL SAFETY EQUIPMENT.

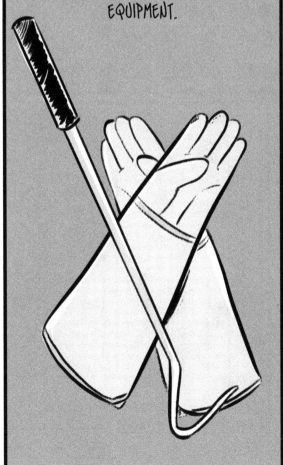

AND SHE COMMONLY LEFT SNAKES' CAGES OPEN TO ALLOW THEM TO CRAWL THROUGHOUT HER WORKSPACE.

THOUGH SHE WAS NOT EVER SERIOUSLY BITTEN DURING HER EMPLOYMENT, HER HABITS BROUGHT HER INTO CONFLICT WITH HER COLLEAGUES AT THE MINNEAPOLIS LIBRARY.

AFTER MUCH PRESSURE, SHE RESIGNED HER POSITION IN 1933.

THE FOLLOWING YEAR SHE BEGAN CURATING REPTILES AT THE BROOKFIELD ZOO OUTSIDE OF CHICAGO.

HOWEVER, HER LAX APPROACH TO SAFETY DID NOT GO OVER WELL WITH THE ZOO STAFF.

AFTER 19 SNAKES ESCAPED UNDER HER CARE, SHE WAS FIRED.

WILEY THEN MOVED TO CALIFORNIA AND FOUND WORK AS A SNAKE TRAINER AND CONSULTANT FOR SEVERAL FEATURE-LENGTH HOLLYWOOD FILMS.

SHE ALSO OPENED A ROADSIDE ZOO IN CYPRESS, CALIFORNIA,

GRACE WILEY REPTILES

...WHERE SHE CHARGED VISITORS 25 CENTS TO SEE HER LARGE PERSONAL COLLECTION.

THEN, ON JULY 20, 1948 SHE INVITED PHOTOJOURNALIST DANIEL P. MANNIX TO HER PROPERTY FOR AN INTERVIEW.

WHILE SHE WAS POSING WITH A NEWLY ACQUIRED INDIAN COBRA, THE FLASH STARTLED THE ANIMAL.

IT LUNGED, AND SHE RESTRAINED IT.

BUT NOT BEFORE BEING BITTEN.

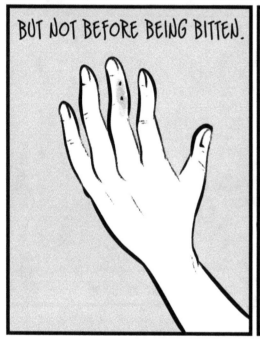

AFTER FINDING HER ONLY VIAL OF COBRA ANTIVENOM BROKEN, SHE WAS RUSHED TO A NEARBY HOSPITAL.

HOWEVER, THE HOSPITAL ONLY HAD ANTIVENOM FOR NORTH AMERICAN SNAKES.

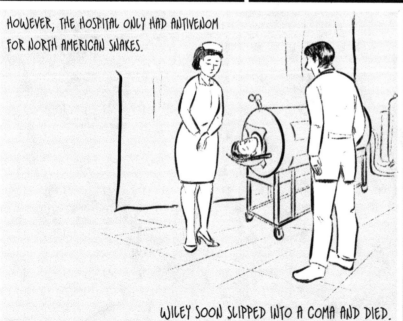

WILEY SOON SLIPPED INTO A COMA AND DIED.

THE SUBJECT OF GRACE OLIVE WILEY'S CAREER AND PASSING STILL PRESENT A POINT OF CONTENTION WITHIN THE HERPETOLOGICAL COMMUNITY TODAY. MANY SAY SHE WAS RECKLESS, AND HER METHODS UNSAFE.

OTHERS, HOWEVER, ASSERT THE RELATIONSHIP SHE HAD WITH HER ANIMALS WAS TRULY UNIQUE, NUTURING AND FASCINATING.

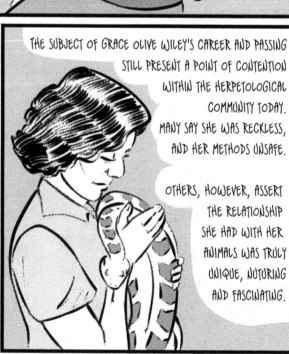

ANIMALS THAT EAT LIGHT!

by KEVIN KITE AND MICHELLE McCAULEY

You look hungry, Fly.

Don't you wish you could photosynthesize like me and eat light?

Yeah, Plant. It isn't fair!

VENU

I can help you with that.

Really?

Come closer. I'll tell you all about it.

Chloroplasts in plant cells absorb energy from sunlight and store the absorbed energy as glucose. The plant cells use glucose to live. That's photosynthesis!

CHLOROPLASTS

As they photosynthesize, chloroplasts in plants release oxygen and water into the atmosphere. Without chloroplasts, life as we know it wouldn't exist on Earth!

O_2

WATER

GLUCOSE

Hmmph! I knew that. But that's plants, Plant! Animals can't do that!

Some animals can...

Whoa! I want that! I could hang out in the sun all day! Tell me how, Plant!

2.4 billion years ago, a single-celled bacterium evolved the ability to photosynthesize for the first time. With the advantage of living off sunlight, these bacteria—we call them cyanobacteria now—multiplied rapidly and eventually made the oxygen-rich atmosphere that allowed animals to evolve.

Cyanobacteria may be the first organisms to photosynthesize, but others followed. About 1 billion years ago, a non-photosynthesizing cell engulfed a photosynthetic cyanobacterium without destroying it. The two organisms had discovered a mutually beneficial arrangement. The engulfed cyanobacteria provided the host cell with glucose, and the host cell provided the cyanobacteria with protection by wrapping it up in a second skin.

Welcome home, Buddy!

Hey! Where's the exit?!?

Eventually, the two organisms managed to coexist, divide, and replicate together, becoming a dynamic duo with a special adaptation! Over millions of years, the entrapped cyanobacteria slowly evolved into our very own chloroplasts. Along the way, though, chloroplasts lost the ability to live independently outside a cell. Now the chloroplast is an organelle within a cell and it needs a host cell to survive.

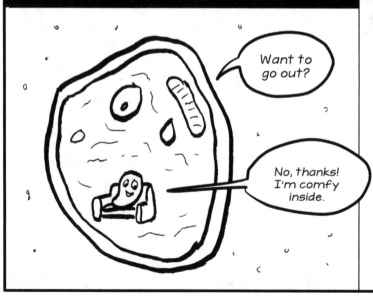

Want to go out?

No, thanks! I'm comfy inside.

This history is why chloroplasts still have their own DNA, separate from the DNA of their host cell—and an important part of my story. Over time, the chloroplast's DNA lost important information about how to make essential proteins that it uses to function and maintain itself. Now, the chloroplast relies on its host cell to make these proteins.

I didn't think this was forever!

You can check out but you can never leave...

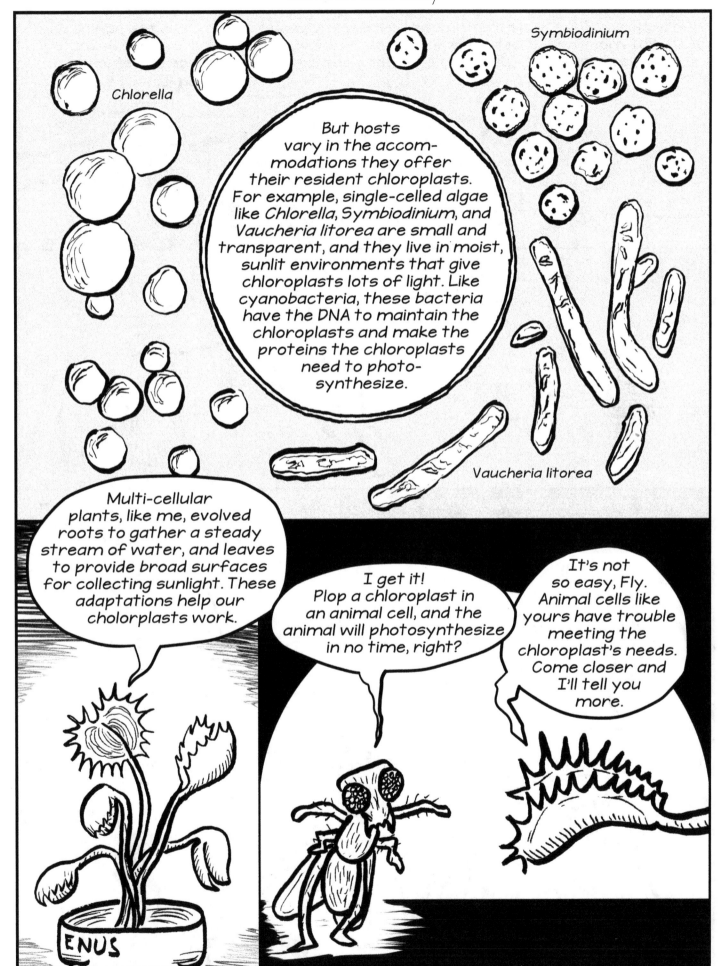

Some animals cooperate with photosynthesizing bacteria. They adapt to form a symbiotic relationship where other organisms benefit the animal. They provide photosynthesizing bacteria with a pleasant, stable, and friendly place to live. The bacteria check in, settle down, and start swapping photosynthesized glucose for light, protection, and a steady supply of CO_2.

The major symbiotic photosynthesizers are the Porifera sponges and the Cnidaria, such as corals, jellyfish, and anemones. These animals all live in water and have bodies full of nooks and crannies that create large surface areas and light-porous skin only two cell layers thick.

Algae like *Chlorella* and *Symbiodinium* wander in and take up residence in the folds and crevices of these animals—the pores and tubules and tentacles and flagella of coral jellyfish, sponges, and anemones serve as safe stable homes for the algae.

Light passes into and through these thin-skinned critters, reaching the algae perched safely inside the animal. The algae take in light, water, and CO_2 and photosynthesize, releasing glucose and carbon, which the animals cells take in.

To be clear, Fly, there's a contract here, and if the animal doesn't provide good conditions, the algae leave, taking photosynthesis with them, causing the animal to "bleach" and starve. This is what happens during the bleaching of coral reefs.

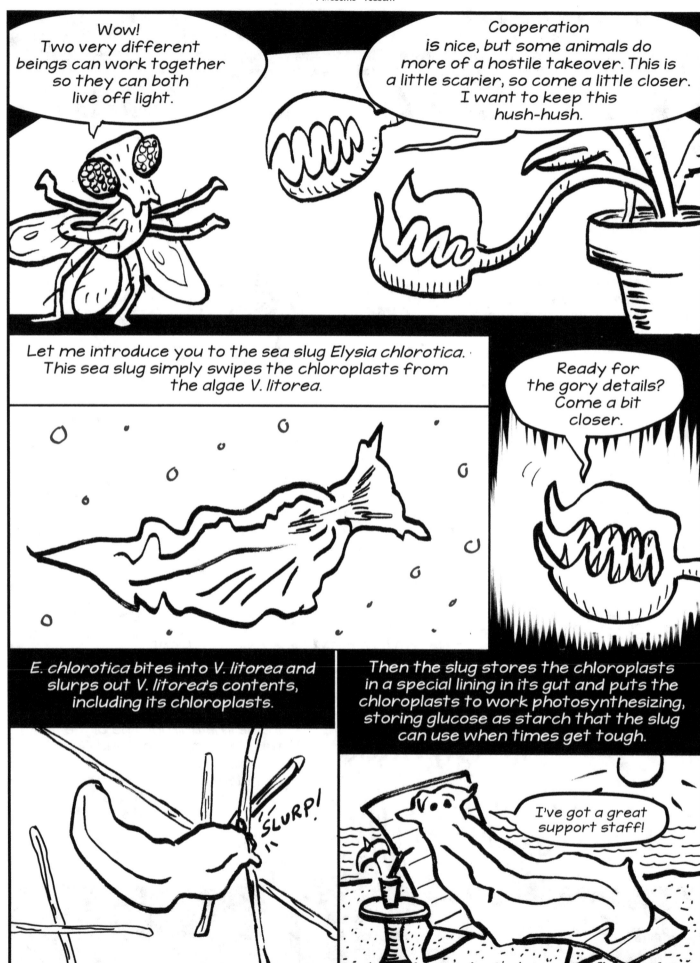

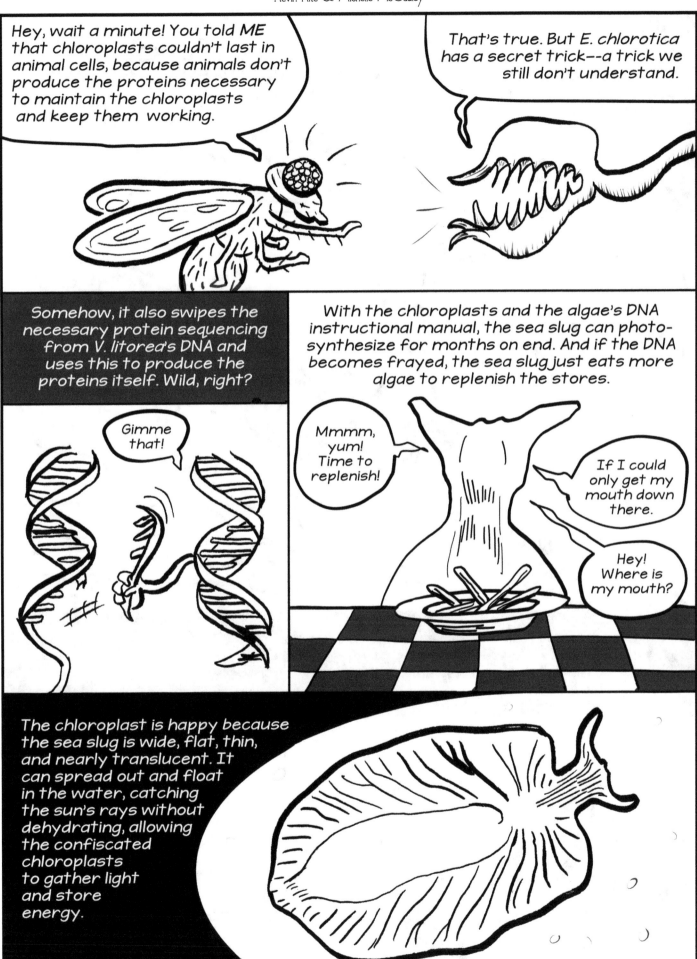

Hey, wait a minute! You told ME that chloroplasts couldn't last in animal cells, because animals don't produce the proteins necessary to maintain the chloroplasts and keep them working.

That's true. But E. chlorotica has a secret trick--a trick we still don't understand.

Somehow, it also swipes the necessary protein sequencing from V. litorea's DNA and uses this to produce the proteins itself. Wild, right?

Gimme that!

With the chloroplasts and the algae's DNA instructional manual, the sea slug can photosynthesize for months on end. And if the DNA becomes frayed, the sea slug just eats more algae to replenish the stores.

Mmmm, yum! Time to replenish!

If I could only get my mouth down there.

Hey! Where is my mouth?

The chloroplast is happy because the sea slug is wide, flat, thin, and nearly translucent. It can spread out and float in the water, catching the sun's rays without dehydrating, allowing the confiscated chloroplasts to gather light and store energy.

OK,
soft, squishy sponges,
jellyfish, and sea slugs can do this.
Sure, they're animals, but they sure
don't look like animals. No legs, eyes,
wings, or anything. Where are the
photosynthesizing crawling
critters? Tell me
about them!

Well . . . the
spotted salamander has
legs and eyes. It doesn't
have wings, but it does have
a backbone. And it's got the
single-celled alga *Oophila
amblystomatis* living inside
it, giving the salamander
its greenish color and
providing its cells with
lovely photosynthesizing
ability.

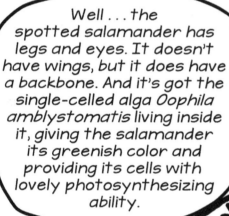

Scientists knew spotted salamander embryos
have a close symbiotic relationship with
O. amblystomatis. The salamander embryos
and the algae are both healthier when they
live together while the embryos are developing.

But scientists discovered that
even when the spotted
salamander grows up,
functioning photosynthesizing
algae live inside its cells
throughout its body.

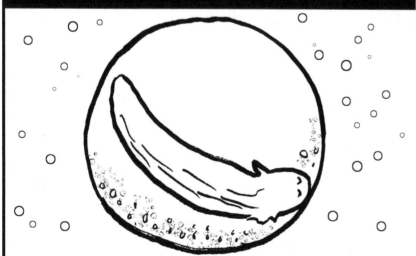

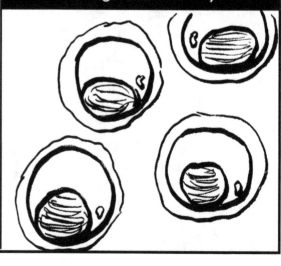

Angela Boyle

A COMIC BY
ALLY SHWED

THE FRIENDSHIP PARK BINATIONAL GARDEN

FROM AN INTERVIEW WITH
DANIEL WATMAN

FRIENDSHIP PARK / EL PARQUE DE LA AMISTAD IS A HISTORIC MEETING PLACE ON THE U.S./MEXICO BORDER OVERLOOKING THE OCEAN.

IN THE U.S., FRIENDSHIP PARK IS LOCATED INSIDE SAN DIEGO'S BORDER FIELD STATE PARK.

IN MEXICO, EL PARQUE DE LA AMISTAD SITS BENEATH A FAMOUS LIGHTHOUSE, EL FARO, ON THE BEACHES OF TIJUANA.

DANIEL WATMAN, A SPANISH TEACHER AND POET, IS THE PRINCIPAL ORGANIZER OF BORDER *ENCUENTRO*.

THIS PROGRAM SEEKS "COMMON INTEREST THEMES" TO BRING PEOPLE TOGETHER THROUGH THE BORDER FENCE.

AS PART OF A 2007 BORDER *ENCUENTRO* ENVIRONMENTAL FESTIVAL, WATMAN AND A TEAM OF STUDENTS AND VOLUNTEERS CREATED THE BINATIONAL GARDEN (JARDÍN BINACIONAL DE LA ARMISTAD)...

...WITH THE ADDED PURPOSE OF PROMOTING NATIVE FLORA.

I HAVE NO BACKGROUND IN NATIVE PLANTS. I HAD TO TALK TO EXPERTS ON BOTH SIDES OF THE BORDER.

I DIDN'T REALIZE HOW MUCH WORK A GARDEN WAS.

I ENDED UP TAKING CARE OF THE GARDEN MOSTLY ON MY OWN... AND LEARNING A LOT!

SO, I'M STILL NEW AT IT.

THE GARDEN WAS A PERFECT THEME FOR COMMON INTEREST ON BOTH SIDES OF THE BORDER. SO I JUST KINDA THOUGHT, NATIVE FLORA.

EVEN IF IT CROSSES TEN FEET OVER THE BORDER, IT'S STILL NATIVE.

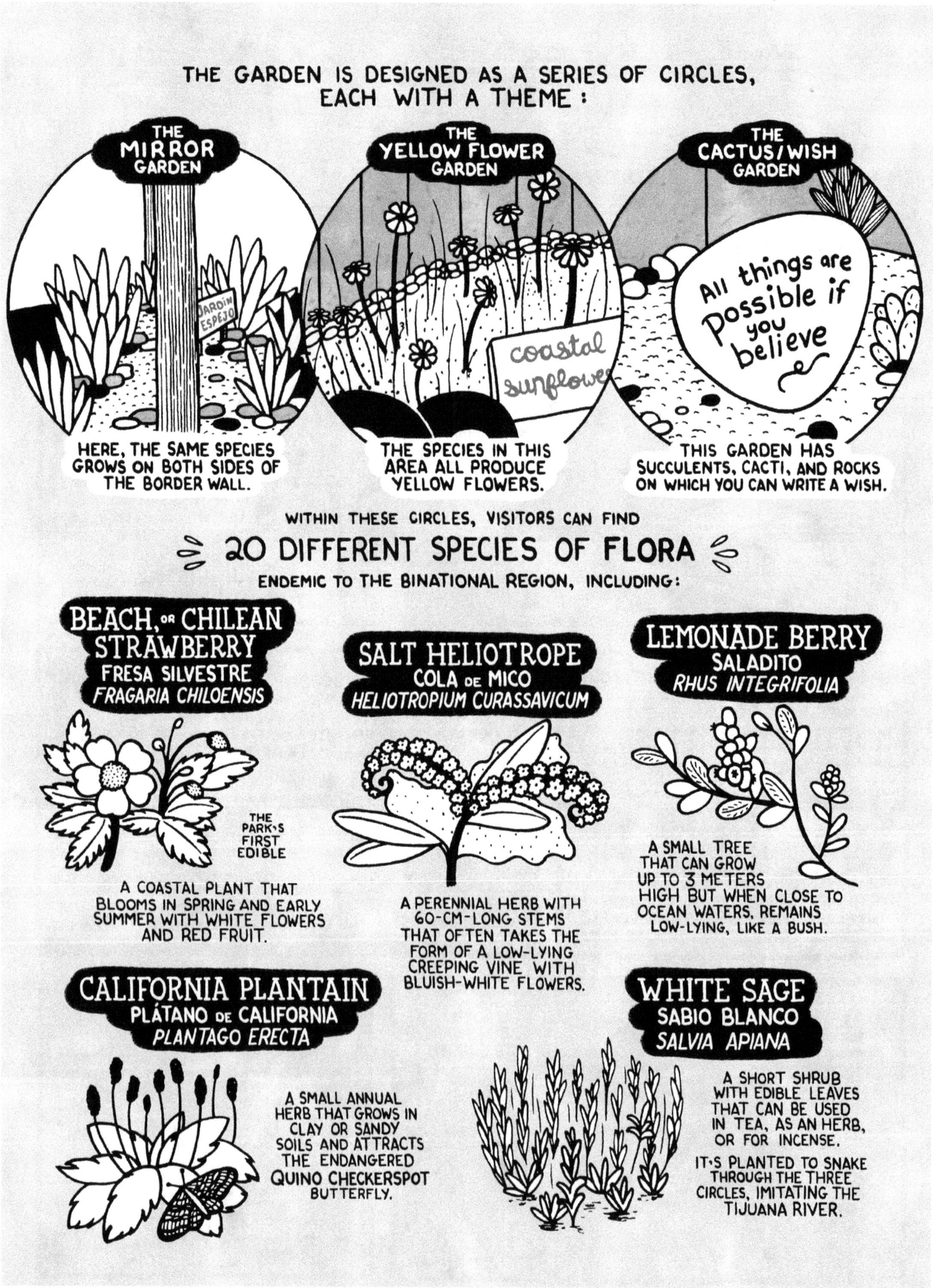

THE GARDEN IS DESIGNED AS A SERIES OF CIRCLES, EACH WITH A THEME:

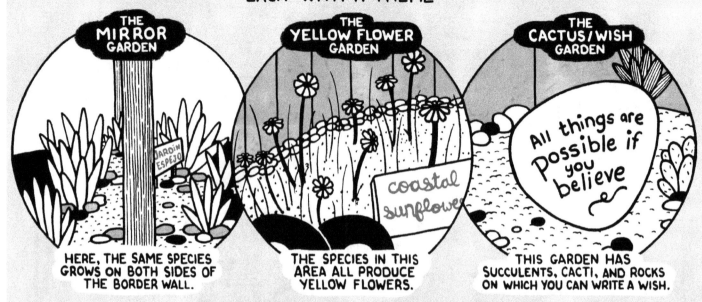

THE MIRROR GARDEN

JARDIN ESPEJO

HERE, THE SAME SPECIES GROWS ON BOTH SIDES OF THE BORDER WALL.

THE YELLOW FLOWER GARDEN

coastal sunflower

THE SPECIES IN THIS AREA ALL PRODUCE YELLOW FLOWERS.

THE CACTUS/WISH GARDEN

All things are possible if you believe

THIS GARDEN HAS SUCCULENTS, CACTI, AND ROCKS ON WHICH YOU CAN WRITE A WISH.

WITHIN THESE CIRCLES, VISITORS CAN FIND

�✑ 20 DIFFERENT SPECIES OF FLORA ✑

ENDEMIC TO THE BINATIONAL REGION, INCLUDING:

BEACH, OR CHILEAN STRAWBERRY
FRESA SILVESTRE
FRAGARIA CHILOENSIS

THE PARK'S FIRST EDIBLE

A COASTAL PLANT THAT BLOOMS IN SPRING AND EARLY SUMMER WITH WHITE FLOWERS AND RED FRUIT.

SALT HELIOTROPE
COLA DE MICO
HELIOTROPIUM CURASSAVICUM

A PERENNIAL HERB WITH 60-CM-LONG STEMS THAT OFTEN TAKES THE FORM OF A LOW-LYING CREEPING VINE WITH BLUISH-WHITE FLOWERS.

LEMONADE BERRY
SALADITO
RHUS INTEGRIFOLIA

A SMALL TREE THAT CAN GROW UP TO 3 METERS HIGH BUT WHEN CLOSE TO OCEAN WATERS, REMAINS LOW-LYING, LIKE A BUSH.

CALIFORNIA PLANTAIN
PLÁTANO DE CALIFORNIA
PLANTAGO ERECTA

A SMALL ANNUAL HERB THAT GROWS IN CLAY OR SANDY SOILS AND ATTRACTS THE ENDANGERED QUINO CHECKERSPOT BUTTERFLY.

WHITE SAGE
SABIO BLANCO
SALVIA APIANA

A SHORT SHRUB WITH EDIBLE LEAVES THAT CAN BE USED IN TEA, AS AN HERB, OR FOR INCENSE.

IT'S PLANTED TO SNAKE THROUGH THE THREE CIRCLES, IMITATING THE TIJUANA RIVER.

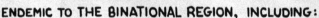

WHEN I FIRST STARTED GETTING INTO IT, I DIDN'T APPRECIATE THE FLORA. IT JUST LOOKED LIKE A BUNCH OF BUSHES.

BUT THEN YOU START TO NOTICE JEWELS HERE AND THERE.

GOLDENBUSH
ISOCOMA MENZIESII

I STARTED TO RECOGNIZE HOW BEAUTIFUL IT IS.

SOME OF MY FAVORITES INCLUDE:

THE JOJOBA, OR GOAT NUT
SIMMONDSIA CHINENSIS

IT LIKES THE ENVIRONMENT AND DOESN'T NEED MUCH WATER. IT HAS A 30-FOOT ROOT SYSTEM BUT GROWS ONLY 5 FEET HIGH. IT'S THE MOST ENDEMIC OF THIS REGION, AND IS PARTICULARLY GOOD FOR THIS ECOSYSTEM BECAUSE OF HOW IT SWAPS NUTRIENTS WITH THE SOIL.

FROM WINTER TO SPRING, YOU CAN SEE ITS LITTLE YELLOW-GREEN FLOWERS, AND IN SUMMER, IT BEARS FRUIT THAT IS USED TO MAKE OIL. IT CAN LIVE FOR OVER 100 YEARS.

AND THE TOYÓN OR CALIFORNIA HOLLY
HETEROMELES ARBUTIFOLIA

IT'S THE OLDEST PLANT IN THE GARDEN, AS WELL AS THE TALLEST: IT CAN REACH A HEIGHT OF UP TO 4 METERS. BUT ON THE U.S. SIDE, WE'RE NOT ALLOWED TO GROW PLANTS TALLER THAN 2 FEET, FOR VISIBILITY PURPOSES WITHIN THE BORDER ENFORCEMENT ZONE.

IT THRIVES ON SLOPED TERRAIN TO OPTIMIZE RAINWATER INTAKE. ITS TINY WHITE AND YELLOW FLOWERS ATTRACT BEES IN AUTUMN, AND IN WINTER GIVE WAY TO CLUSTERS OF RED FRUIT.

IN A BLOG POST FROM 2010, DAN REFLECTED:

THE MORE TIME I SPENT WITH THE PLANTS, THE MORE I STARTED TO FEEL LIKE WE WERE CARING FOR EACH OTHER.

I IMAGINED THE $O_2 - CO_2$ LIFE CYCLE WORKING DIRECTLY ON ME AS I EXPELLED WHAT FELT LIKE NEGATIVE ENERGY, KNOWING THAT THEY TAKE IN AND NOURISH WHAT I LET OUT, AND I GAIN LIFE FROM THE OXYGEN THEY PRODUCE.

I ALWAYS FINISHED WITH A MORE *calm & tranquil* PERSPECTIVE ON LIFE.

IT WAS QUITE THERAPEUTIC.

COASTAL AGAVE
AGAVE SHAWII

PRESENTLY, YOU CAN ACCESS THE GARDEN ON THE U.S. SIDE — WITH PERMISSION FROM THE BORDER PATROL AGENT ON DUTY DURING REGULAR PARK VISITING HOURS.

OPEN Sa·Su
10AM-2PM

IF YOU VOLUNTEER TO WORK IN THE GARDEN, ACCOMPANIED BY DAN, YOU MAY BE ABLE TO ACCESS THE AREA FOR LONGER.

IT'S A BIT DIFFERENT ON THE MEXICAN SIDE, WHICH IS OPEN 24 HOURS A DAY, 7 DAYS A WEEK.

IN THE COURSE OF A YEAR, ABOUT 100 PEOPLE VOLUNTEER IN TIJUANA, VERSUS 12-20 PEOPLE ON THE U.S. SIDE.

AS A COALITION, WE'RE WORKING TO PROMOTE A TRULY BINATIONAL PARK WITH NO WALLS.

THAT'S OUR FOCUS NOW.

I'VE STARTED DOING THESE PICNICS NEXT TO THE BORDER, RIGHT NEXT TO DONALD TRUMP'S PROTOTYPES FOR BORDER WALLS.

WE'RE PROTOTYPING FRIENDSHIP.

DAN SAYS MAINTAINING THE GARDEN IS A CONSTANT STRUGGLE.

FOR EXAMPLE, NEAR THE END OF 2011, THE U.S. BORDER PATROL WAS PREPARING FOR A NEW PRIMARY BARRIER.

A TEAM OF LANDSCAPE ARCHITECTS, NATIVE PLANT EXPERTS, GARDENERS, AND VOLUNTEERS HAD TO REMOVE AND STORE THE PLANT IN NURSURIES ON EITHER SIDE OF THE BORDER.

BUT THIS GAVE THEM THE OPPORTUNITY TO CREATE THE NEW DESIGN THAT NOW EXISTS WITHIN THE CIRCLES, BISECTED BY THE NEW BARRIER.

REGARDLESS OF WALLS, IT IS ONE GARDEN THAT BELONGS TO THE PEOPLE OF BOTH TIJUANA AND SAN DIEGO, AS OPPOSED TO TWO SEPARATE GARDENS ON EITHER SIDE.

The environment doesn't have any borders.

— DANIEL WATMAN

LOCATED OFF THE EAST COAST OF AFRICA, MADAGASCAR IS AN ISLAND WITH A RICH ECOSYSTEM.

BAD LUCK LEMUR

MOSS Bastille

BECAUSE OF THE ISLAND'S ISOLATION, MANY UNIQUE SPECIES HAVE EVOLVED THAT ARE FOUND NOWHERE ELSE.

madagascar

CUCKOO ROLLER

PANTHER CHAMELEON

FOSSA

HISSING COCKROACH

EVEN AMONG THESE MANY REMARKABLE LIFEFORMS, ONE CREATURE STANDS OUT...

THE AYE-AYE, *DAUBENTONIA MADAGASCARIENSIS.*

LEMUR FAMILY REUNION

DUE TO ITS STRANGE APPEARANCE, SCIENTISTS FIRST CLASSIFIED IT AS A RODENT. HOWEVER, IT WAS EVENTUALLY DISCOVERED TO BE A TYPE OF LEMUR, WHICH MAKES IT A PRIMATE AND A DISTANT COUSIN TO HUMANS.

THE AYE-AYE POSSESSES A COMBINATION OF TRAITS THAT SETS IT APART FROM OTHER PRIMATES.

IT HAS LARGE EARS AND SHARP TEETH THAT GROW CONTINUOUSLY, LIKE A RODENT'S, AND MUST BE CONSTANTLY WORN DOWN. BUT THE AYE-AYE'S MOST REMARKABLE FEATURE IS ITS LONG AND SKELETAL MIDDLE FINGER.

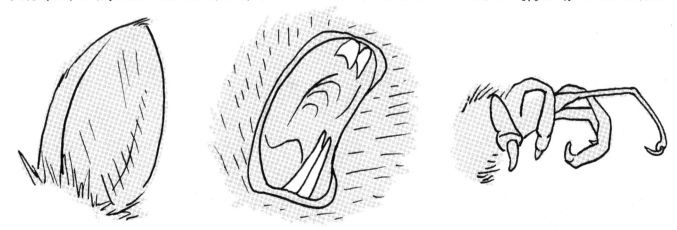

THE AYE-AYE HAS EVOLVED AN UNUSUAL METHOD OF HUNTING, CALLED "PERCUSSIVE FORAGING." USING ITS SPECIALIZED FINGER, IT TAPS RAPIDLY ON TREE BARK.

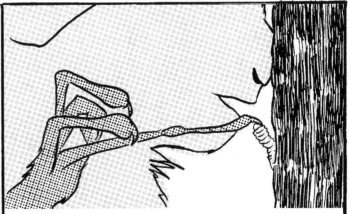

WITH ITS KEEN HEARING, IT LISTENS FOR ECHOES MADE BY INSECT LARVAE HIDING IN THE WOOD. THEN IT TEARS A HOLE IN THE BARK WITH ITS TEETH AND HOOKS THEM OUT.

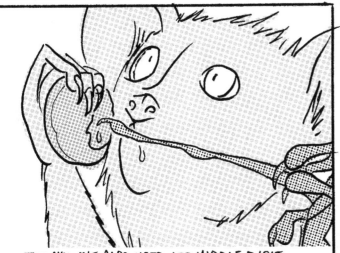

THE AYE-AYE ALSO USES ITS MIDDLE DIGIT FOR A VARIETY OF OTHER PURPOSES, SUCH AS EATING FRUIT OR EGGS.

IN ADDITION, IT IS USED AS A "TOILET CLAW" FOR GROOMING.

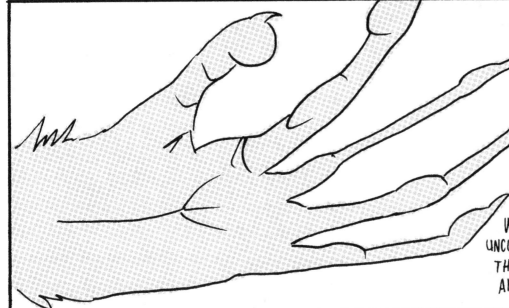

SCIENTISTS HAVE FOUND THAT THE AYE-AYE'S MIDDLE FINGER REMAINS 6°C (43°F) COLDER THAN ITS OTHER DIGITS WHEN NOT IN USE. THE REASON IS UNCLEAR, BUT IT MAY SAVE ENERGY. THE FINGER WARMS UP AS THE ANIMAL HUNTS NOCTURNALLY.

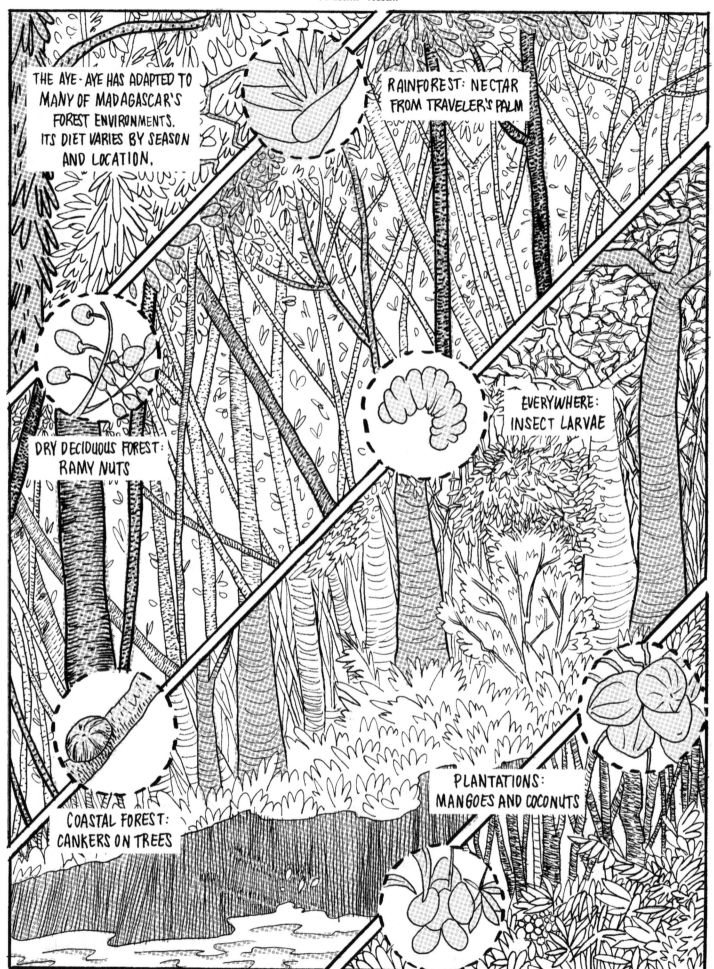

THE AYE-AYE HAS ADAPTED TO MANY OF MADAGASCAR'S FOREST ENVIRONMENTS. ITS DIET VARIES BY SEASON AND LOCATION.

RAINFOREST: NECTAR FROM TRAVELER'S PALM

EVERYWHERE: INSECT LARVAE

DRY DECIDUOUS FOREST: RAMY NUTS

PLANTATIONS: MANGOES AND COCONUTS

COASTAL FOREST: CANKERS ON TREES

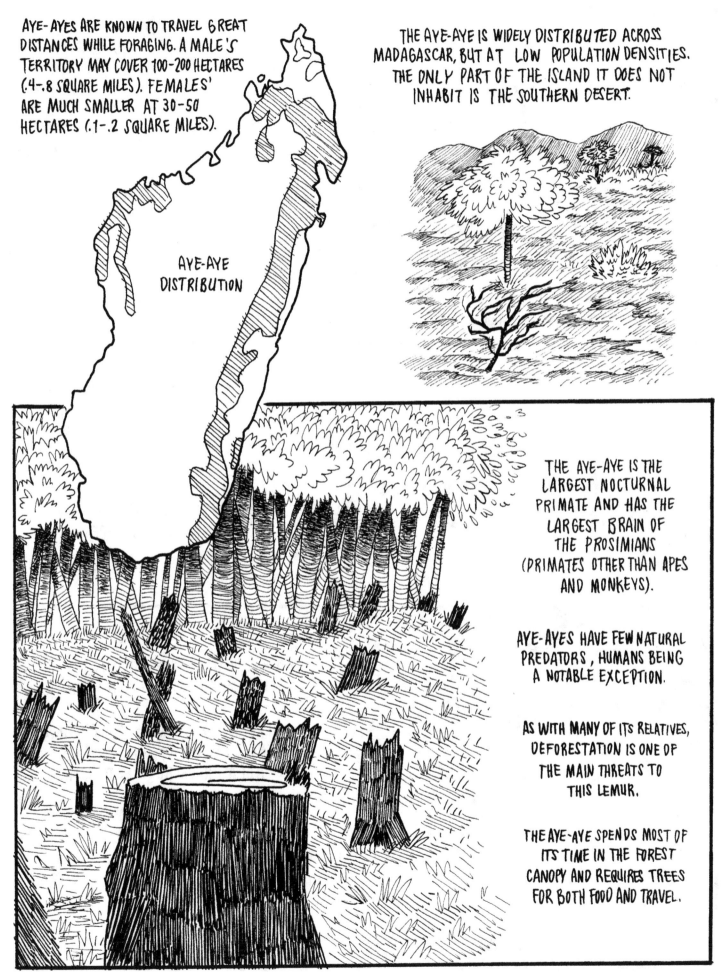

AYE-AYES ARE KNOWN TO TRAVEL GREAT DISTANCES WHILE FORAGING. A MALE'S TERRITORY MAY COVER 100-200 HECTARES (.4-.8 SQUARE MILES). FEMALES' ARE MUCH SMALLER AT 30-50 HECTARES (.1-.2 SQUARE MILES).

AYE-AYE DISTRIBUTION

THE AYE-AYE IS WIDELY DISTRIBUTED ACROSS MADAGASCAR, BUT AT LOW POPULATION DENSITIES. THE ONLY PART OF THE ISLAND IT DOES NOT INHABIT IS THE SOUTHERN DESERT.

THE AYE-AYE IS THE LARGEST NOCTURNAL PRIMATE AND HAS THE LARGEST BRAIN OF THE PROSIMIANS (PRIMATES OTHER THAN APES AND MONKEYS).

AYE-AYES HAVE FEW NATURAL PREDATORS, HUMANS BEING A NOTABLE EXCEPTION.

AS WITH MANY OF ITS RELATIVES, DEFORESTATION IS ONE OF THE MAIN THREATS TO THIS LEMUR.

THE AYE-AYE SPENDS MOST OF ITS TIME IN THE FOREST CANOPY AND REQUIRES TREES FOR BOTH FOOD AND TRAVEL.

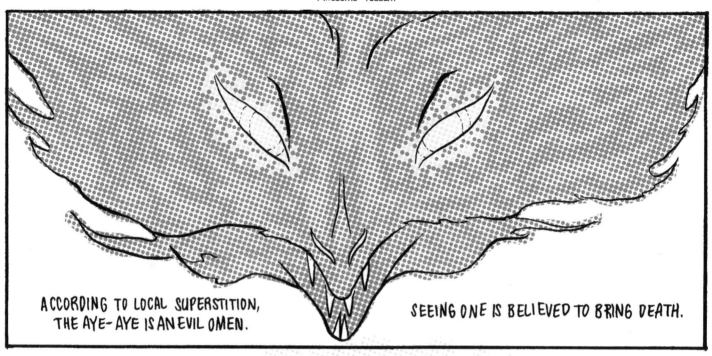

ACCORDING TO LOCAL SUPERSTITION, THE AYE-AYE IS AN EVIL OMEN.

SEEING ONE IS BELIEVED TO BRING DEATH.

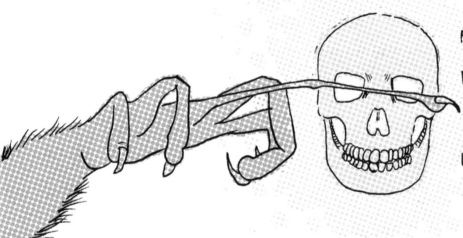

FOLKLORE OF THE MALAGASY PEOPLE ALSO SAYS THAT IF AN AYE-AYE POINTS AT YOU WITH ITS MIDDLE FINGER, YOU WILL DIE.

SOME EVEN SAY THAT IT CREEPS INTO HOUSES AT NIGHT TO PIERCE THE HEARTS OF SLEEPERS.

BECAUSE OF THESE SUPERSTITIONS, THE ANIMAL IS OFTEN KILLED ON SIGHT.

HOWEVER, THERE HAVE BEEN MANY CONSERVATION EFFORTS SINCE THE 1950s, AND SEVERAL PROTECTED AREAS HAVE BEEN ESTABLISHED.

ALTHOUGH IT IS LISTED AS ENDANGERED, SEVERAL BREEDING CENTERS HAVE BEEN SET UP AROUND THE WORLD. THERE IS A MOVEMENT TO BRING MORE AWARENESS TO THIS SINGULAR SPECIES, WHICH HAS BEEN MISUNDERSTOOD FOR SO LONG.

ADULT
MOTHS

♀ ♂

PUPA/
COCOON

INVASIVE NOMADS:
THE
GYPSY MOTH
Lymantria dispar

EGG
MASS

CATERPILLAR/LARVA

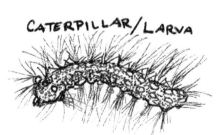

BY KAMI KOYAMATSU

There once was a Frenchman named Leopold Trouvelot.

He lived in Medford, Massachusetts where he painted portraits.

Trouvelot was also an amateur entomologist with an interest in breeding silkworms.

Massachusetts

France

In 1869, Trouvelot decided to bring European gypsy moths to North America from France with hopes to breed the gypsy moths with silkworms. His goal was to cultivate a silkworm that was less susceptible to predation.

He incubated the egg masses on a tree in his back yard.

Buff color

In spring the eggs hatched into little caterpillars.

Gypsy moth caterpillars prefer oak but will also eat other deciduous tree leaves.

Gypsy moth caterpillars can spin a silken thread allowing them to disperse on the wind.

When Trouvelot noticed some of the larvae had escaped, he quickly notified authorities

whoops...

But nothing was done...

After the incident Trouvelot decided to pursue astronomy instead of entomology.

He was particularly interested in the sun, published many papers, and created illustrations for the Harvard College Observatory.

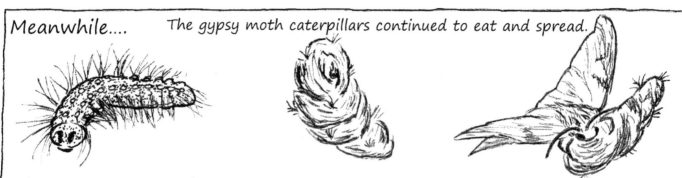

Meanwhile.... The gypsy moth caterpillars continued to eat and spread.

When they are two months old, gypsy moth caterpillars spin a cocoon and become pupae. Then two weeks later they emerge as adult moths.

A female European gypsy moth cannot fly. Instead, she releases a pheromone and waits for a hunky man moth to come find her.

Female gypsy moths are about 5-6 cm,

white with brown zig-zag markings.

Male gypsy moths are usually around 3 ½ - 4 cm with mottled brown markings.

The males spend their days flying around in search of females.

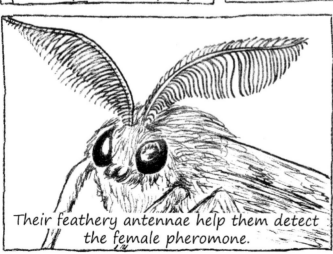

Their feathery antennae help them detect the female pheromone.

Adult gypsy moths do not eat; they spend all of their time trying to find each other to make moth babies.

Once hanky-panky has been successful, the female gypsy moth lays her egg mass, thus restarting the cycle of moth life and continued invasion.

One egg mass can contain up to 1,000 eggs.

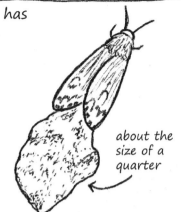

about the size of a quarter

In 1882, the first gypsy moth outbreak in North America was in Medford, Massachusetts.

Coincidentally, this was the same time that Trouvelot moved back to France.

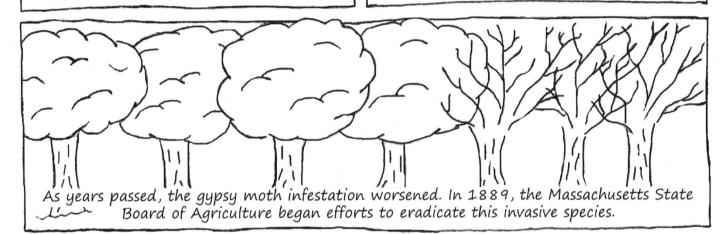

As years passed, the gypsy moth infestation worsened. In 1889, the Massachusetts State Board of Agriculture began efforts to eradicate this invasive species.

They tried manually removing egg masses, burning down infested forests, and applying primitive insecticides.

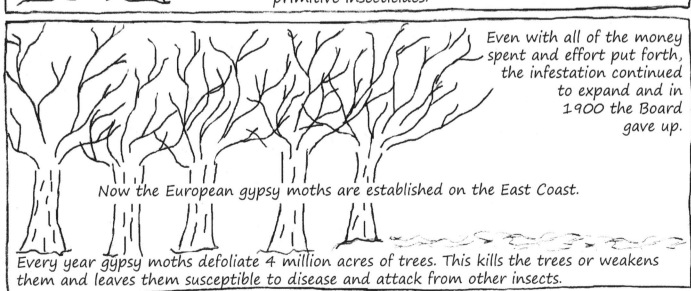

Even with all of the money spent and effort put forth, the infestation continued to expand and in 1900 the Board gave up.

Now the European gypsy moths are established on the East Coast.

Every year gypsy moths defoliate 4 million acres of trees. This kills the trees or weakens them and leaves them susceptible to disease and attack from other insects.

European gypsy moths are continuing to spread across the continent.

Female gypsy moths can lay eggs on ANY outdoor surface, including bird houses, lawn furniture, vehicle wheel wells, tarps, and more!

When someone moves from an infested area they may unknowingly transport eggs to an uninfected area.

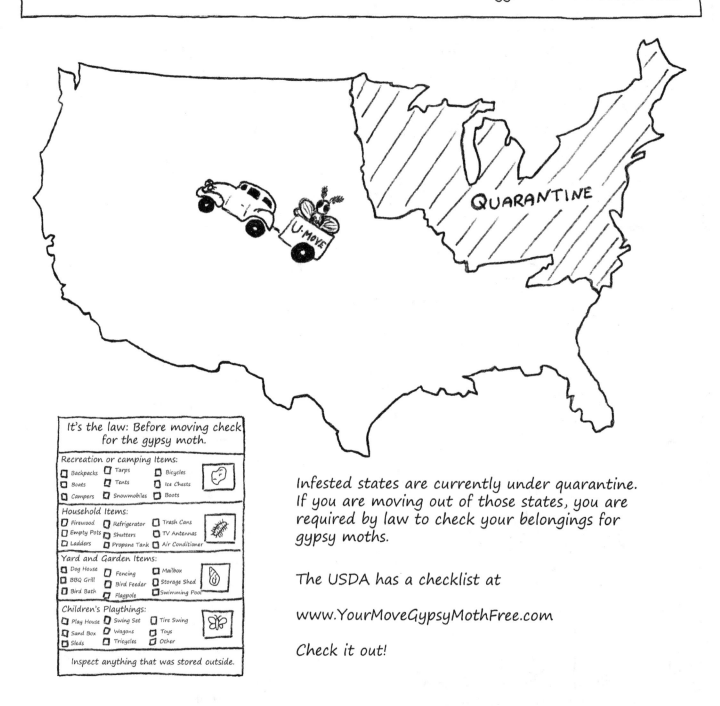

QUARANTINE

It's the law: Before moving check for the gypsy moth.

Recreation or camping Items:
- Backpacks
- Boats
- Campers
- Tarps
- Tents
- Snowmobiles
- Bicycles
- Ice Chests
- Boots

Household Items:
- Firewood
- Empty Pots
- Ladders
- Refrigerator
- Shutters
- Propane Tank
- Trash Cans
- TV Antennas
- Air Conditioner

Yard and Garden Items:
- Dog House
- BBQ Grill
- Bird Bath
- Fencing
- Bird Feeder
- Flagpole
- Mailbox
- Storage Shed
- Swimming Pool

Children's Playthings:
- Play House
- Sand Box
- Sleds
- Swing Set
- Wagons
- Tricycles
- Tire Swing
- Toys
- Other

Inspect anything that was stored outside.

Infested states are currently under quarantine. If you are moving out of those states, you are required by law to check your belongings for gypsy moths.

The USDA has a checklist at

www.YourMoveGypsyMothFree.com

Check it out!

BUT WAIT, THERE'S MORE!

There is a second gypsy moth species, the Asian gypsy moth!

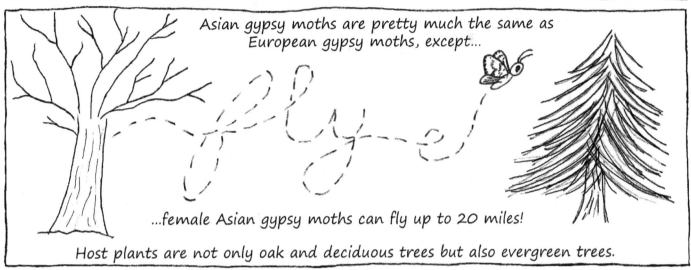

Asian gypsy moths are pretty much the same as European gypsy moths, except...

fly

...female Asian gypsy moths can fly up to 20 miles!

Host plants are not only oak and deciduous trees but also evergreen trees.

Asian gypsy moths come across the ocean on shipping containers traveling from infested areas in Asia and Europe.

And still, these female gypsy moths can also lay their eggs on ANY outdoor surface!

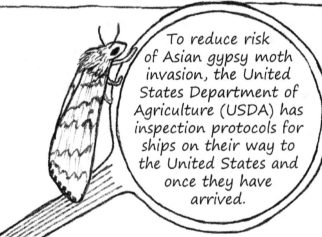

To reduce risk of Asian gypsy moth invasion, the United States Department of Agriculture (USDA) has inspection protocols for ships on their way to the United States and once they have arrived.

Because of the flight risk and broader host range, Asian gypsy moths can be even more devastating than their European counterparts.

WHAT IS CURRENTLY BEING DONE?

Well, for example, the Washington State Department of Agriculture (WSDA) has been trapping and eradicating gypsy moth since 1974.

Trappers set out traps with the female pheromone, which attracts the males.

When the not-so-brilliant men find the traps, they enter thinking they have found some sweet, sweet love.

Instead they become stuck.

Washington State

Knowing where male gypsy moths are helps to locate where an infestation is underway.

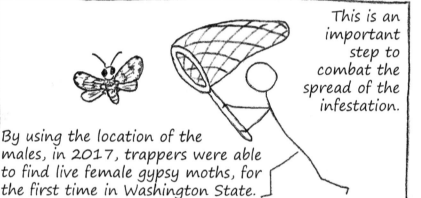

This is an important step to combat the spread of the infestation.

By using the location of the males, in 2017, trappers were able to find live female gypsy moths, for the first time in Washington State.

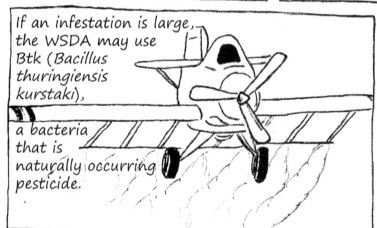

If an infestation is large, the WSDA may use Btk (*Bacillus thuringiensis kurstaki*),

a bacteria that is naturally occurring pesticide.

The USDA is working with state and local governments to suppress the spread of and to eradicate gypsy moth.

WHAT CAN YOU DO?

Be friendly to gypsy moth trappers, give them a nice wave, and welcome them to place a trap in your yard.

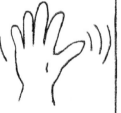

If you find a gypsy moth, contact your local Department of Agriculture for proper identification and removal.

If you are moving, make sure you inspect ALL of your outdoor items. Say "No!" to hitchhikers!

If you find an egg mass, scrape it off into a container and pour boiling water onto it. Just scraping the mass onto the ground will do nothing.

If you find a gypsy moth caterpillar or adult moth, squash the mother bugger.

But be careful, skin contact with the caterpillars can cause allergic reactions, including itchy rashes.

There are many native species of moths in the United States that are often mistaken for gypsy moths.

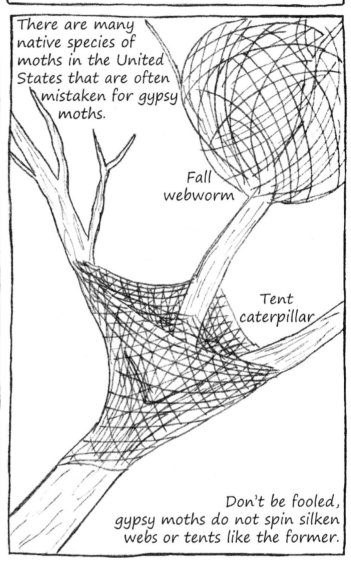

Fall webworm

Tent caterpillar

Don't be fooled, gypsy moths do not spin silken webs or tents like the former.

Gypsy moths are the only caterpillars with red and blue spots. They can grow to be 7 cm long and have dark hairy bodies.

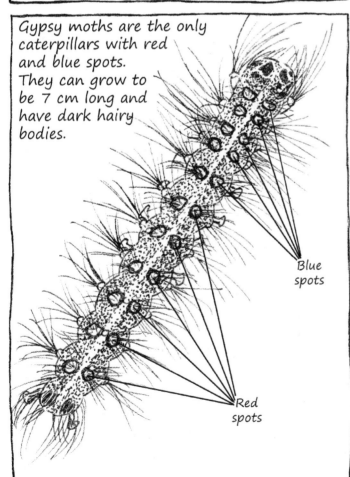

Blue spots

Red spots

The moral of the story is: gypsy moths are not your friends.

And never introduce an exotic species, however small, to a new area.

Elisa Järnefelt

Fantastic *Ficus*, Full of Figs

by Angela Boyle

You know the ficus in the office corner. The "fig" in Fig Newtons. Same plant. Well, same genus.

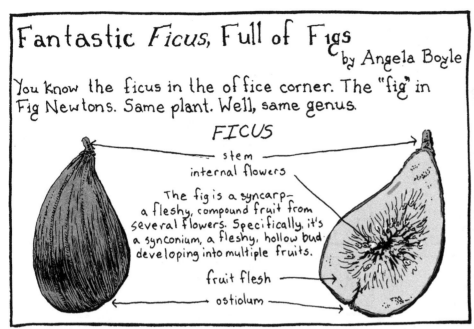

FICUS

stem
internal flowers

The fig is a syncarp— a fleshy, compound fruit from several flowers. Specifically, it's a synconium, a fleshy, hollow bud developing into multiple fruits.

fruit flesh

ostiolum

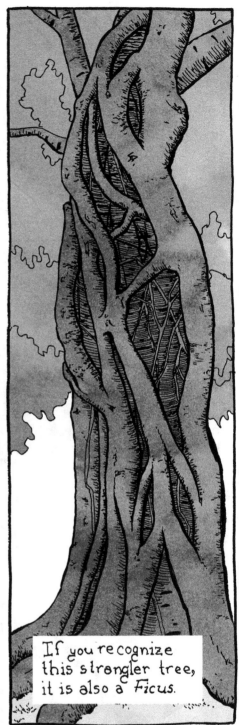

If you recognize this strangler tree, it is also a *Ficus*.

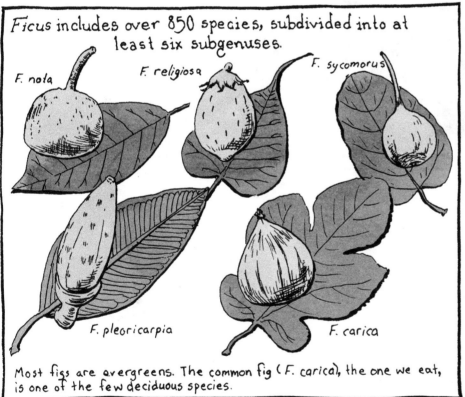

Ficus includes over 850 species, subdivided into at least six subgenuses.

F. nota

F. religiosa

F. sycomorus

F. pleoricarpia

F. carica

Most figs are evergreens. The common fig (*F. carica*), the one we eat, is one of the few deciduous species.

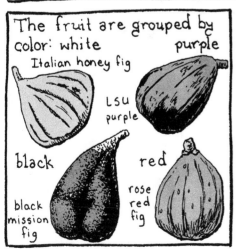

The fruit are grouped by color: white — purple

Italian honey fig

LSU purple

black

red

black mission fig

rose red fig

Figs also come in a variety of shapes: round — turbinate — egg-like — ribbed — pear-shaped

F. maxima

F. septica

F. auriculata

F. cummaronis

F. rubignosa

Shape is a good part of the fig's delight.
—JANE GRIGSON, English cookery writer

Ficus reproduce through a unique technique. They coevolved with the fig wasp, their pollinator.

F. rubignosa

This is a ripe fig.

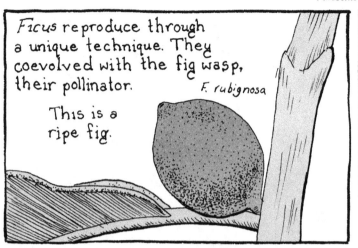

This wasp has been flying for miles on air drifts, covered in pollen from the fig she was born in.

Searching for a whiff of ripe fig

Pleistodontes imperialis

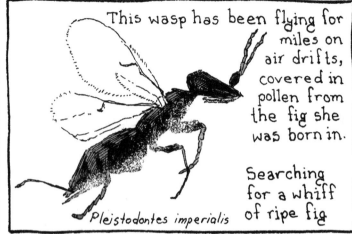

Upon finding that ripe fig,

she enters through the ostiolium.

The ostiolium is so small that...

...it pulls her wings off. She can never leave

Fun Facts: Only the corresponding species of fig wasp will pollinate a specific fig species. Some parasitic fig wasps can get inside. And only the females of the fig wasp can fly.

Once inside, she lays her eggs in the flowers.

Then, like a salmon,

she dies.

As the fig ripens, the eggs start to hatch.

The males hatch first. They inseminate the females still inside the fig flowers.

Eventually, the females also hatch—winged, pregnant, and ready to go.

By this stage, the fig is ripe, and the thin skin has likely cracked open.

The males dig their way out of the fig.

NOM NOM NOM

The females follow the males outside, covered in pollen.

After all that hard work,

the males die quickly

after leaving the fig.

The female drifts away, searching for a whiff of her new fig. Though poor fliers, some species can travel up to 20 miles away, the longest distance for any pollinator.

Once she finds her new fig, she starts the cycle anew.

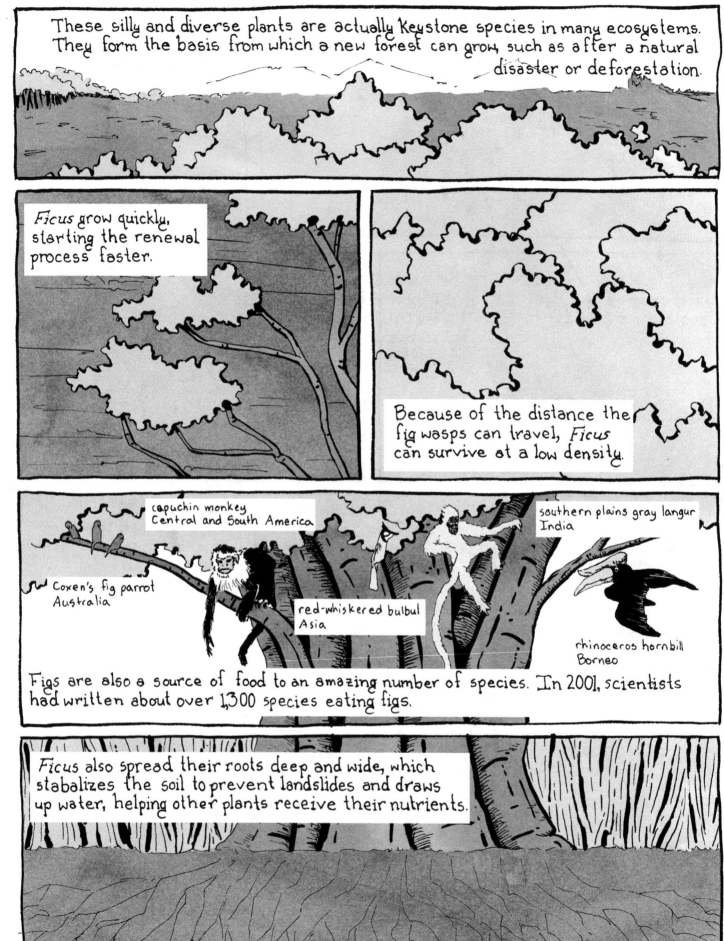

These silly and diverse plants are actually keystone species in many ecosystems. They form the basis from which a new forest can grow, such as after a natural disaster or deforestation.

Ficus grow quickly, starting the renewal process faster.

Because of the distance the fig wasps can travel, Ficus can survive at a low density.

capuchin monkey
Central and South America

southern plains gray langur
India

Coxen's fig parrot
Australia

red-whiskered bulbul
Asia

rhinoceros hornbill
Borneo

Figs are also a source of food to an amazing number of species. In 2001, scientists had written about over 1,300 species eating figs.

Ficus also spread their roots deep and wide, which stabalizes the soil to prevent landslides and draws up water, helping other plants receive their nutrients.

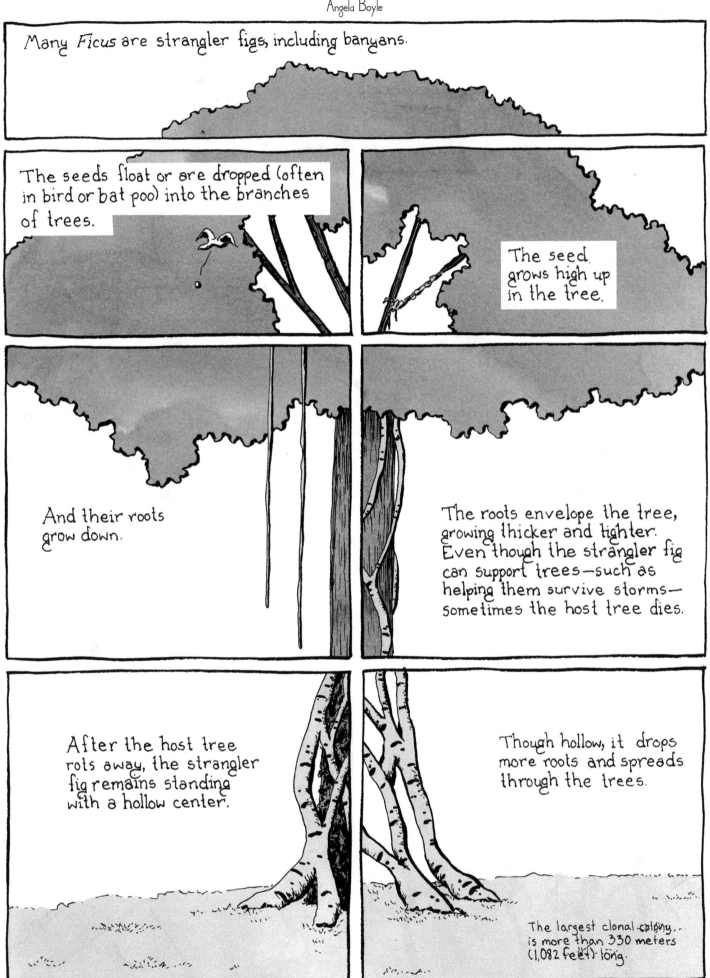

Many *Ficus* are strangler figs, including banyans.

The seeds float or are dropped (often in bird or bat poo) into the branches of trees.

The seed grows high up in the tree.

And their roots grow down.

The roots envelope the tree, growing thicker and tighter. Even though the strangler fig can support trees—such as helping them survive storms—sometimes the host tree dies.

After the host tree rots away, the strangler fig remains standing with a hollow center.

Though hollow, it drops more roots and spreads through the trees.

The largest clonal colony is more than 330 meters (1,082 feet) long.

In 2006, figs were found in Lower Jordan Valley, indicating the fig might be the earliest plant cultivated by humans.

The figs were dried (for storage) and seedless. (they could only grow more trees from cuttings.)

Abandoned around 11,200 years ago, the figs in Lower Jordan Valley are 1,000 years older than when we thought people were growing crops.

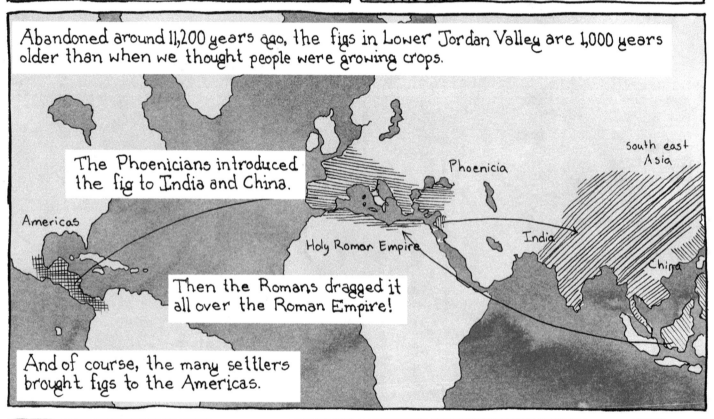

The Phoenicians introduced the fig to India and China.

Then the Romans dragged it all over the Roman Empire!

And of course, the many settlers brought figs to the Americas.

South east Asia

Phoenicia

Americas

Holy Roman Empire

India

China

The Greeks held the fig in high esteem, naming villages after it. Even forbidding it's export.

Americans cultivated four horticultural figs. These species do not require pollination, (because the fig wasps can't live in North America).

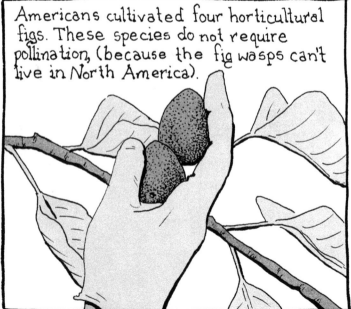

There are many famous fig trees throughout history, religion, and literature. Ashvattha is the world tree in Hindu mythology, a supernatural *F. religiosa*.

In Homer's *Odyssey*, Odyssyeus is saved from falling into Charybdis, the whirlpool monster, by grabbing the branch of a fig tree (*F. carica*), which droop down right above the monster.

NOM NOM NOM

Jaya Sri Maha Bodhi (*F. religiosa*) is the oldest human-planted tree on record, in 288 BCE. In Sri Lanka, it is supposedly a branch from the tree under which Buddha attained enlightenment.

The largest known specimen is "Auntie Sarah's Banyan," an *F. microcarpus* in Kauai, Hawaii.

33 meters tall

crown spread: 76 meters

over one thousand aerial trunks

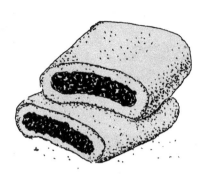

If you think figs are good only
for seed-filled Newtons or overly
fancy bacon-wrapped figs, the most
traditional human food can't be limited
to just these simple options.

Figgy pudding, from the old
Christmas carol is baked,
steamed, boiled, or fried.
It was originally made with figs
and dates back to sixteenth
century England. Here's a sticky
figgy pudding with a home-made
caramel sauce.

**Fig and goat
cheese pizza** is
a new spin and
usually includes
caramelized
onions.

Preheat oven to 450°.
Make or buy 1lb. of dough and roll out to 1in.
  thick. In some sort of shape. Place on
  a pan dusted in corn meal.
Spread 1Tb olive oil on the dough.
Spread 5oz. goat cheese, 4 to 6 figs (cut
  in half, cut-side up), and caramelized
  onions (from 1 small sweet onion) around.
Top with ½c mozzarella.
Bake 15 to 20min.

Put in a saucepan: 2c dried figs, 2c
  water. Bring to a boil.
Remove from heat and add 1tsp baking
  soda. Let cool 5 min and then puree.
Beat together: 7Tbp butter and 1c sugar.
  Add 2 eggs and beat well.
Fold in 2.5c self-rising flour, then the
  puree, then 2.5oz grated dark chocolate.
Put this in eight 1c ramekins and bake
  for 20 to 25 min.
Create a caramel sauce by mixing 2c
  brown sugar, 2c heavy cream, and 14Tbp
  butter over low heat. When sugar
  dissolves, bring to a boil, then lower and
  simmer for 5 min.
When the ramekins come out, let them
  sit 5min. Cut across the top of puddings
  and pour the sauce in. Then pour more
  sauce all over all of them and allow it
  to soak.
Top with fresh figs, quartered, and ice
  cream or whipped cream. Serve warm.

Fig chutney is
served as a
condiment on
roasted meat or
with cheese

Bring to a boil: 2½c red wine vinegar, ½lb.
  light brown sugar, 1 chopped onion, ¼c
  chopped ginger, 1½tp mustard seeds,
  zest of ¼ lemon, ½ cinnamon stick,
  1¾ tp salt, ¼ tp allspice, ⅙ tp clove.
Simmer until reduced by ⅓.
Add 1¼ lb. firm, fresh figs and cook until
  almost falling apart (30 min).
Store in a glass container up to 3 weeks
  in the refridgerator.

Farm to Bust:
Natural History and Ecology of the 1930s Dust Bowl

Hatty Koerner

The time and place: 1930s North American Great Plains

In order to understand what led to the 1930s we go back...way back.

The problem: drought, dust storms, starvation.

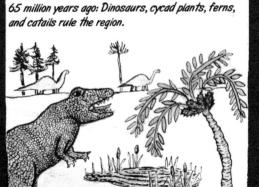

65 million years ago: Dinosaurs, cycad plants, ferns, and catails rule the region.

Saurophaganax and Apatosaurus dinosaurs

55 million years ago: The Rocky Mountains form gradually, creating a large dry rain shadow. Strong winds prevent trees from growing.

In the semi-arid climate, grass species flourish.

10,000 years ago: Humans Arrive: Apache, Sious, Blackfoot, Kiowa, and Comanche Tribes hunt buffalo.*

150 years ago: This delicate ecosystem still contains features of its geological past. The Native American tribes practice hunting, gathering, and non-invasive farming methods.

The interdependence of plants, animals and humans create a sustainable enviornment.

Native grasses grow on a rich, fertile layer of topsoil and deposit nutrients.

Underneath the topsoil, a different kind of soil with a high percentage of clay lies. Soil scientists, later call it "loess soil," and now believe it is deposited by centuries of wind.

Most soil in Eastern North American and in Europe is loam soil, which contains higher nutrient content, sand, and silt.

Saurophaganax fossil

*Horses became part of triabl cultures a mere 500 years ago after Spanish Conquistadors imported them. Tribal clothes have changed over time, and vary by tribe. I based this drawing after an undated picture of a Comanche man.

Native Grasses of the Great Plains

Tallgrass Prairie Plants

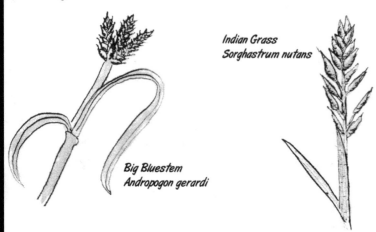

Indian Grass
Sorghastrum nutans

Big Bluestem
Andropogon gerardi

Within the Great Plains, a variety of ecosystems exist.

Tallgrass prairies are charcterized by plants that range between 1 and 3 meters. Shortgrass prairies contain much shorter grasses, usually growing only a 1/3 meter, or 1 foot, high.

When European explorers first entered the prairies, the landscape seemed so alien to them that they called the prairies, "inland seas."

European explorers came to consider many of the native species as simple weeds. This belief has lasting consequences- few large areas of native plants are left to appreciate and study. Most prairie land is now agricultural.

Shortgrass Prairie Plants

Blue Grama
Bouteloua gracilis

Buffalograss
Bouteloua dactyloides

Sideoats grama
Bouteloua curtipendula

Keystone Animal Species

Robert Paine, a professor of zoology at the University of Washington, developed the idea of keystone species in 1969. A keystone species is one that plays an important role in balencing the ecosystem.

Two keystone species of the prairies are prairie dogs and American bison.

Around 1900, people start moving to the prairies to set up homesteads.

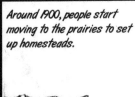

Crops grow, farmers make money. World War I demand inflates crop prices. Many farming families come with little but quickly prosper.

Critics worry that distance and climate will make the Plains difficult to farm.

Politicans and poor, hopeful farmers prefer not to listen.

Scientists and journalists popularize the mistaken view of climate science, "rain follows the plow."

At first rain does come. Word of opportunity spreads, more settlers come.

Families go into debt to buy land, tractors.

In the 1920s, buying on credit is easy.

New, diesel powered tractors plow more land.

But farmers don't understand the enviornmental consequences.

As it would turn out, the 1910s and 1920s had been exceptionally wet.

In the 1930s, arid conditions return. Strong winds blow away topsoil, exposing loess soil. Crops blow away.

At first farmers plant more crops to compensate.

By 1934, dust storms, "black blizzards," sweep across the Plains.

Dust pneumonia kills livestock and human beings.

In 1935, dust storms reach as far as Washington, D.C., and Chicago.

Settlers are faced with a choice: stay put or leave. Many families, deep in debt and struggling to survive, choose to leave. They go West, mostly on Route 66 to California. In Canada they go North.

One migrant recalls leaving: "I got a lasting mental picture of the little home...

..standing lonely and silent now, with the mice playing in the rooms."

The other choice is staying.

This means hoping that somehow, someday, things will get better.

Many of the people who stay survive off government assistance. Food and jobs are scarce.

Throughout the 1930s, the world experiences economic depression.

Crop prices drop; high debts and dust storms offer no relief for farmers.

Some politicans advocate "laisse faire" economics, hoping time will help.

The New Deal: The Agricultural Adjustment Act, 1933

Franklin O. Roosevelt

X Signature

President Roosevelt signs

legislation known as the "New Deal."

The New Deal starts subsidy payments to farmers. These payments allow farmers to let some fields lie fallow. Fallow fields mean less supply and higher prices.

The bill creates the Soil Conservation Service, SCS, a federal agency tasked with scientifically investigating the causes of erosion.

Under the New Deal, farmer education programs prevent land misuse. Farmers stop over planting corn and wheat because they drain the soil of nutrients.

From the SCS: Contour plowing uses the natural contours of the earth to plant. This method reduces erosion.

SCS researches plants that prevent erosion. Farmers are taught to plant fallow fields with nitrogen fixing plants. That way, the following year the crops will have more nutrients and grow strong and healthy, thus producing better yields.

A variety of plants are used to prevent erosion and ensure healthy soil.

Windbreaker trees prevent eroison.

Hairy vetch is a nitrogen fixing crop cover that can be planted on fallow fields.

New methods of farming, soil conservation, and anti-erosion species cannot bring back the native plants or fertile top soil destroyed by dust storms and intensive farming of 1920s.

New, introduced species help restore equiillibrium to the land.

Fairway Grass: A hybrid anti-erosion plant.

The story of fairway grass's invention spans two continents and three countries:

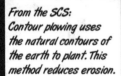

The original seeds of fairway grass came from a variety of grasses found on the Russian steppes.

Russian scientists sent seeds to Moscow for further research.

The seeds made their way from Moscow, to the Unitd States, and then to Canada. At the University of Saskachewan, the agronomist L. E. Kirk uses them to invent an anti-erosion hybrid, fairway grass. Fairway grass is planted all over North America in areas prone to erosion.

Despite all the scientific innovations that have made it possible to continue farming in the Great Plains....

The most difficult part of fixing farming practices in North America involves changing a mentality deeply ingrained in farming ethos: the profit motive.

Many farmers are driven by the hope of a richer future.

New appreciation of conservation plays a role in ending the Dust Bowl. The field of ecology brings disparate scientists together to understand the region.

Aldo Leopold
1887- 1948

The writer and biologist Aldo Leopold promotes respect for the land. The US Congress cites Leopold, acknowledging the importance of "mutual interdependent cooperation between human animals, other animals, plants and the soils."

In Leopold's own writing, he goes further than the US Congress, implicating business cycles and material excess, "The priority of industry has become dogma....
Do we realize that industry, which has been our good servant, might make a poor master?"

WHILE TIGERS AND SHARKS RULE LAND AND WATER, EAGLES RULE THE SKIES, I THINK. THEY ARE BEAUTIFUL AND MAJESTIC CREATURES. THEY CAN GROW LARGE, BUT THE LARGEST EAGLE TO EVER EXIST WAS THE

HAAST'S EAGLE

THE HAAST'S EAGLE (*HARPAGORNIS MOOREI*) WAS THE BIGGEST, BADDEST, AND MOST MAGNIFICIENT EAGLE TO HAVE EVER EXISTED.

THEY COULD WEIGH UP TO 17.8 KG. AND HAD A WINGSPAN OF UP TO 3 MT.

BY SHASHWAT MISHRA

H. MOOREI USED TO LIVE IN THE SOUTH ISLANDS OF NEW ZEALAND DURING THE 1400.

THE EAGLE HAD A PROPORTIONALLY LARGE HEAD, BILL, LEGS, AND TALONS.

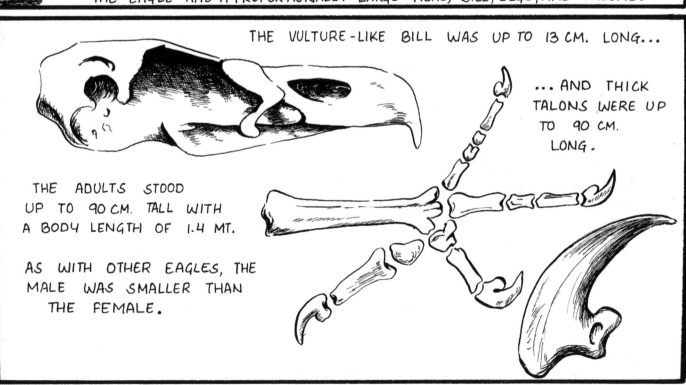

THE VULTURE-LIKE BILL WAS UP TO 13 CM. LONG...

...AND THICK TALONS WERE UP TO 90 CM. LONG.

THE ADULTS STOOD UP TO 90 CM. TALL WITH A BODY LENGTH OF 1.4 MT.

AS WITH OTHER EAGLES, THE MALE WAS SMALLER THAN THE FEMALE.

THE BIRD GETS ITS NAME AFTER DR. JULIUS VON HAAST, WHO DISCOVERED REMAINS OF THE BIRD IN 1871.

ONE STUDY ESTIMATED THE TOTAL PREHISTORIC POPULATION AT 3,000-4,500 BREEDING PAIRS.

THEIR LIFESPAN IS BELEIVED TO HAVE BEEN ABOUT 20 YEARS. THESE EAGLES, IN PAIRS, OCCUPIED SEVERAL HUNDRED SQUARE KILOMETERS. THEY WEREN'T ADAPTED FOR SOARING HIGH IN THE SKY BUT STAYED LOW, FLYING AMONG TREES.

NOW, LET'S MOVE TO A MORE INTERESTING PART- HUNTING.

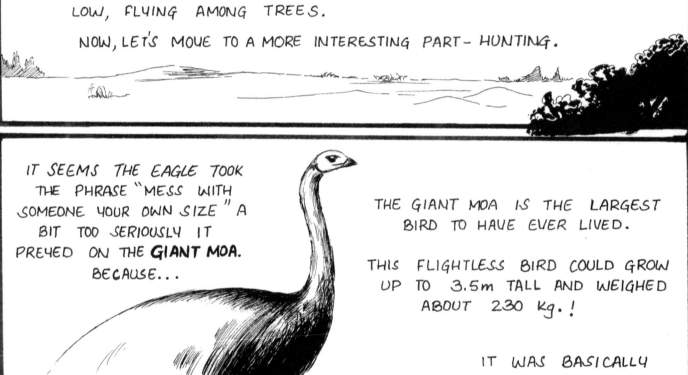

IT SEEMS THE EAGLE TOOK THE PHRASE "MESS WITH SOMEONE YOUR OWN SIZE" A BIT TOO SERIOUSLY IT PREYED ON THE **GIANT MOA**. BECAUSE...

THE GIANT MOA IS THE LARGEST BIRD TO HAVE EVER LIVED.

THIS FLIGHTLESS BIRD COULD GROW UP TO 3.5m TALL AND WEIGHED ABOUT 230 kg.!

IT WAS BASICALLY LIKE A GIANT OSTRICH.

AND THE HAAST EAGLE MADE THESE THEIR PRIMARY PREY.

AS HAS BEEN THEORIZED, THE EAGLE WOULD SIT PERCHED AT AN ELEVATED POSITION AND ON SPOTTING A MOA...

...WOULD SWEEP DOWN AT SPEEDS OF UP TO 80 Kmph...

...HITTING THE MOA LIKE A CINDER BLOCK FROM AN EIGHT STOREY BUILDING...

...WITH ITS HUGE, SHARP TALONS.

MARKS FOUND ON MANY MOA SPINES AND NECK BONES SUGGEST THAT'S WHERE THE HAAST'S EAGLE WOULD STRIKE THE PARALYZING BLOW.

AND DAMAGE FOUND TO THE MOA'S PELVIS BONES SUGGEST THAT THE EAGLE'S BILL WAS LONG ENOUGH TO REACH THE KIDNEYS.

AS IS TOO OFTEN THE CASE, EXTINCTION OF THE EAGLE WAS BECAUSE OF THE ADVENT OF HUMAN BEINGS.

ABOUT 500-600 YEARS AGO, THESE ISLANDS OF NEW ZEALAND WERE INHABITED BY A TRIBE CALLED MAORI.

THE MAORI'S HUNTED DOWN THE GIANT MOA.

AS THE MOA POPULATION DWINDLED, SO DID THE EAGLE'S... TO EXTINCTION.

BOTH THE HAAST AND MOA EVOLVED D TO SUCH A SIZE DUE TO A PHENOMENON CALLED 'ISLAND GIGANTISM'... WHERE ANIMALS ISOLATED FROM OTHER, MORE DIVERSE POPULATIONS OF ANIMALS, END UP A MUCH LARGER SIZE THAN THEY'D BE ON THE MAINLAND.

DUE TO A LACK OF MAMMALS, THE HAAST'S EAGLE BECAME THE ISLAND'S APEX PREDATOR.

THE LARGEST EAGLE TO EVER EXIST WAS DESCRIBED BY THE MAORI TO HAVE HAD RED, BLACK, AND WHITE PLUMAGE WITH BLACK FEATHERS TINGED WITH YELLOW AND GREEN WITH A BUNCH OF RED FEATHERS ON ITS HEAD.

BUT, ALAS, WE'LL NEVER SEE THE BIRD OURSELVES.

As you can see, I have some distinctive features.

So sit back and I'll tell you a bit about why I'm so unique.

MY, WHAT HAIRY EARS YOU HAVE

BY KELLY L. SWANN

But first, let me introduce myself.

My scientific name is *Caracal caracal.*

I am a caracal, a wild cat found in Africa, the Middle East, and India.

155

Compared to other wild cats, my size may not instantly scream, "A threat!"

In fact, if I'm domesticated you might even be able to pick me up.

But I do have a feature which makes me a huge threat.

No, not wings.

My powerful hind legs allow me to lunge and leap, enabling me to catch birds mid-flight.

I can jump high.

3 meters

Though I don't have to leap up; I've been known to kill and eat a sitting ostrich. Yes, I know they're large, but my jaws are strong.

I don't mind feathers, but birds aren't all I eat. These are but a sample of my diet:

pouched mouse

young kudo

vervet monkey

red-billed francolin

black-lined plated lizard

little buttonquail

springhare

hyrax

hare

I eat feathers but cut off stiff hair before I eat mammals.

dik-dik

springbok

mongoose

SO WHAT'S UP WITH MY EARS?

You humans have come up with
a few ideas...

FLY SWATTER—
Are they designed to keep pesky flies away?

CAMOUFLAGE—
Do my ear tufts help disguise
me in tall grass?

COMMUNICATION—
Is "talking" with other caracals
my ears' primary purpose?

ENHANCED HEARING—
Or do they mainly help
me zero in on my prey?

Maybe some day you'll know for sure, but until then,
I think it's time for lunch...

The liger is the largest living species of cat in the world. The largest liger on record grew to be more than 3.5 m in length and 418.2 kg.

LIGERS AND OTHER HYBRIDS

By Tom O'Brien

Although the liger is an impressive animal, they don't exist in the wild because they are a hybrid.

A hybrid is the result of combining the qualities of two organisms of different breeds, varieties, species, or genera. In the instance of a liger, a male lion and a female tiger, making it's scientific name *Panthera leo* ♂ x *Panthera tigris* ♀.

P. Leo   x   P. tigris

Lion   Tiger

Often the genders of the species of the parents have an effect on what type of hybrid is born. For example, if a female lion and a male tiger were to breed, the result would be a tigon.

P. leo   x   P. tigris

Lion   Tiger

Tigon

Hybridization is a delicate process for most animals and is uncommon in the wild.

HYBRIDIZATION

FRAGILE

The territory of tigers and lions don't overlap outside of zoos, so neither ligers nor tigons occur in the wild.

Liger
Breed in
Captivity

At one point in time the territory of the Asiatic lion did overlap with the territories of the Bengal tiger and the Caspian tiger, so it is possible that ligers and tigons did exist in the wild at one point.

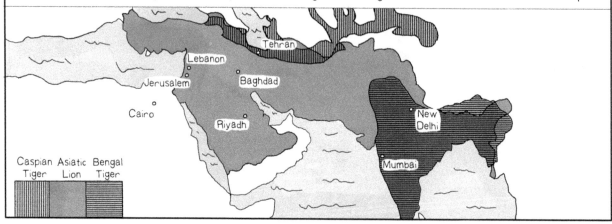

Tehran
Lebanon
Jerusalem
Baghdad
Cairo
Riyadh
New Delhi
Mumbai

Caspian Tiger   Asiatic Lion   Bengal Tiger

Physical location isn't the only barrier to hybridization though. Different physiology, breeding seasons, behaviors, cues for mating, and a host of other factors all impact two species ability to breed.

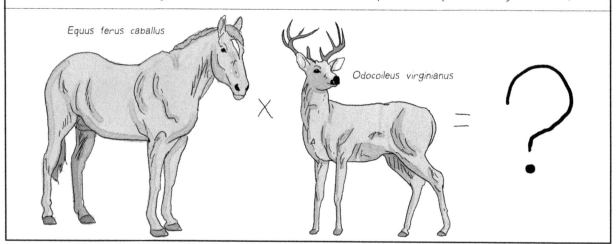

Equus ferus caballus

Odocoileus virginianus

X   = ?

One of the biggest barriers to hybridization is the fact that some cross-breeding animals have different chromosome counts, so their DNA is often incompatable.

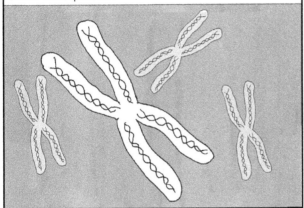

For example, the mule is a hybrid of a male donkey (62 chromosomes) and a female horse (64 chromosomes). As a result, mules have 63 chromosomes which make their births rare and also makes them sterile.

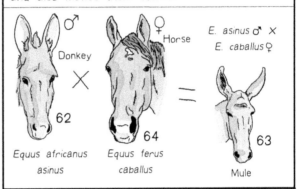

Donkey ♂
62
Equus africanus asinus

Horse ♀
64
Equus ferus caballus

E. asinus ♂ X
E. caballus ♀

63
Mule

However, some hybrid animals and plants have stable genetic structures which allow for them to continue reproducing. These hybrids are often the start of a new species. One example of this is the red wolf, a cross between the gray wolf and the coyote.

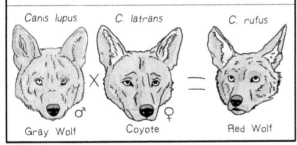

Canis lupus
C. latrans
C. rufus

Gray Wolf ♂
Coyote ♀
Red Wolf

Many hybrids though are unstable or sterile and never reproduce themselves.

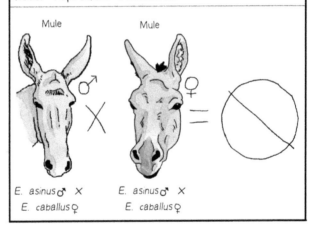

Mule ♂
Mule ♀

E. asinus ♂ X
E. caballus ♀

E. asinus ♂ X
E. caballus ♀

Ligers were long considered to be sterile, and although male ligers are, in 2012 a female liger managed to breed with a male lion, creating a liliger. The two had cubs again in 2013.

P. leo ♂ x
P. tigris ♀

P. leo

Liger ♀
Lion ♂

Hybridization is also known as crossbreeding and is an important aspect in the genetic modification of crops as well as the development of new breeds and species of animals.

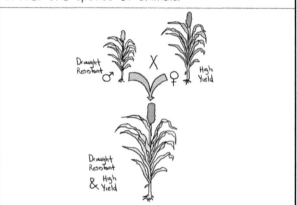

Although hybridization is difficult in animals, it is relatively common and easy in plants.

Recent crop modification has used hybridization to make crops with higher yields, with insect resilience that requires fewer pesticides, that handle drought better, and that require less fertilizer, among other things.

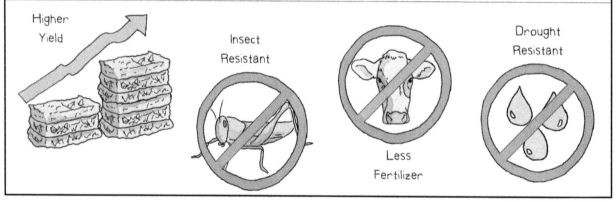

Examples of common hybrid crops include sweet corn, Meyer lemons, and Durum wheat.

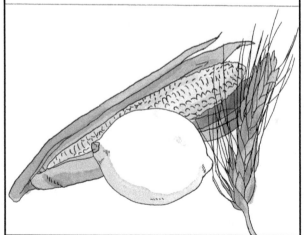

Be it a liger or a new strain of high-yield wheat, hybrids exist and thrive in our world.

FARLEY AND THE WOLVES

Farley Mowat was a Canadian naturalist and prolific author. He published 45 books, many on the relationship between humans and nature.

He passed away at the age of 92 in 2014.

Farley cared deeply about animals.

From my first consciousness I have been closely connected to the rest of animate creation—

the non-human element, as well as the human.

This theme of emotional connection has earned him some critism from the scientific community for anthropomorphising his subjects of study. Like Jane Goodall, he named them with human names and described their personalities.

He has also been accused of outright lying.

Farley's approach to critism was to make light of it.

I never let the facts get in the way of truth.

This quote is similiar to the remarks of Mark Twain.

Never let facts get in the way of a good story.

His literary explorations included the native tribes of Canada, whaling, and arctic animals.

However today we're going to be looking at his work *Never Cry Wolf*, published in 1963.

Farley was hired by Canada's Dominion Wildlife Service to investigate dwindling caribou and deer populations, with the implication that wolves were to blame.

In *Never Cry Wolf*, he talks to a Chief whose predecessor was fired for suggesting that humans were responsible for the diminished herds.

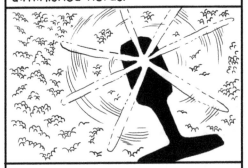

Nevertheless, Farley traveled to Keewatin.

He set up camp and shortly thereafter met a pack of wolves forming a family unit.

Angeline

George

Uncle Albert

the pups

Early on he began to notice a strange behavior—the wolves were spending a lot of time hunting mice and other small mammals.

This posed the question—could a wolf live on such a diet? Farley tested the theory on himself.

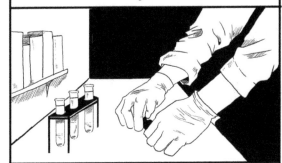

And later, he began to study wolf scat, finding mouse bones present.

He also studied humans, speaking to an Inuit man named Ootek.

The caribou feeds the wolf, but it is the wolf that keeps the caribou strong.

We know that if it were not for the wolf there would be no caribou at all . . .

This idea deeply contrasted with the Canadian belief that wolves had an insatiable blood lust and hunted caribou, livestock, and human alike indescriminately.

Both the Inuit and Canadians hunted caribou to feed themselves and their sled dogs. Farley estimated that as many as 112,000 deer were hunted each year, dwarfing earlier estimates.

Combined with his studies on diet, he concluded that humans were responsible for the dwindling herds.

We have doomed the wolf not for what it is but for what we deliberately and mistakenly percieve it to be:

the mythologized epitome of a savage, ruthless killer—which is, in reality, not more than the reflected image of ourselves.

We have made it a scapegoat for our sins.

Never Cry Wolf was adapted by Disney into a film of the same name in the year 1983.

Disney's movie helped spread Farley's empathetic portrayal of wolves as a necessary predator in nature.

Ideas like introducing more wolves into Yellowstone National Park were no longer met with resistance.

(The project has increased the region's populations of beaver, willow trees, and songbirds.)

United States Vice Presidential Candidate and resident of Alaska Sarah Palin was faced with great opposition when she proposed bills that would make it legal to claim a bounty on each wolf killed.

And when a wolf cull was proposed in 2015 in British Columbia, then-Conservation Director Ian McAllister condemned the action.

The government is not moving forward to protect adequate amounts of habitat to save the caribou; they're instead using wolves as a scapegoat and planning just a horrific level of aerial killing in the coming months. This is truly a war on wolves in British Columbia.

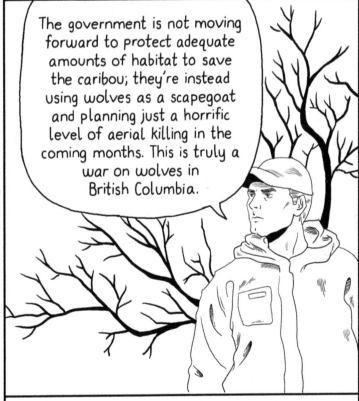

His comments reflect Farley's sentiments.

However, we have begun to see the adverse effects of this friendship between people and wolves. Within Vancouver's Pacific Rim Park, some residents have fed the native wolves.

As a result, they are becoming habituated, attacking dogs and humans alike.

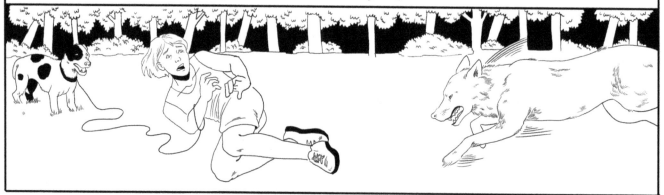

The balance of hominids and canines is delicate and necessary for the survival of expansive populations living in forests around the globe.

Farley Mowat stressed that humans do not live outside the ecosystem of this world, and that our actions affect it. In *Never Cry Wolf* and his other books, he urged us to examine our impact and take responsibility for our actions.

Their coloration is meant to camouflage them into their surroundings.

Males and females have different appearances which is known as *sexual dimorphism*.

Plumage indicating the chicks' sex appear around six weeks.

This plumage allows a family to blend into the grass to hide from predators.

And other predators, both avian and mammalian.

Buteo

Western Cottonmouth

Racoon

Coyote

Like Cooper's hawk.

Since they can't fly very far, Bobwhites will remain in families, or coveys, for safety.

Illustrations

DISAPPEARING RIVER?

The A'ay Chu River once ran a 15 mile course originating in the Kaskawulsh Glacier and emptying into the southern corner of Kluane Lake.

In the spring of 2016 the Kaskawulsh Glacier retreated causing the A'ay Chu River to drastically shrink, all but disappearing over the course of a few days, leaving dry, dusty mudflats in it's place.

Researchers have since attributed the change in the river's flow to man-made climate change.

Lauren Norby

Kelly L. Swann

Amphibians of
BLACK COUNTRY

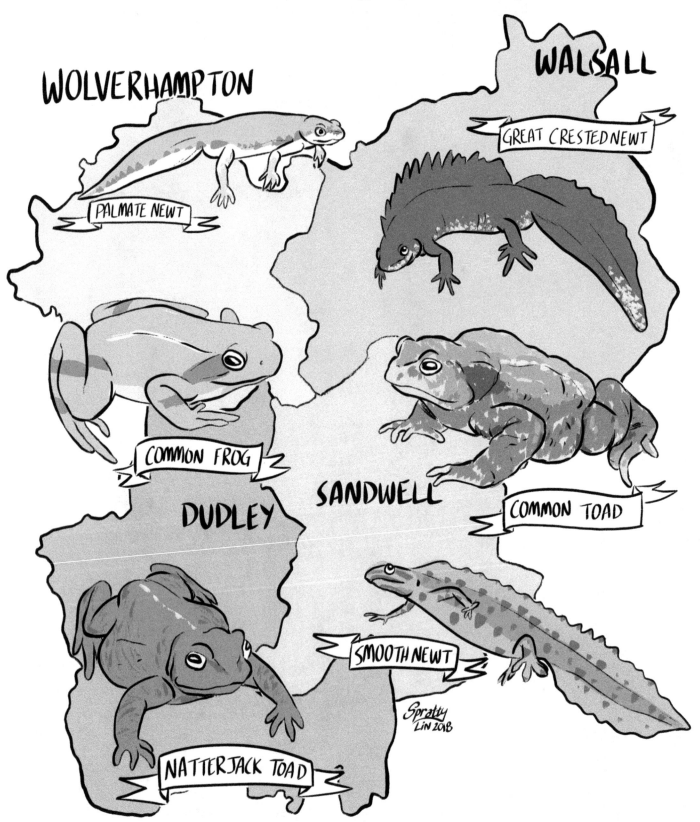

WOLVERHAMPTON

WALSALL

GREAT CRESTED NEWT

PALMATE NEWT

COMMON FROG

COMMON TOAD

SANDWELL

DUDLEY

SMOOTH NEWT

Spratty
Lin 2018

NATTERJACK TOAD

Bridget Comeau

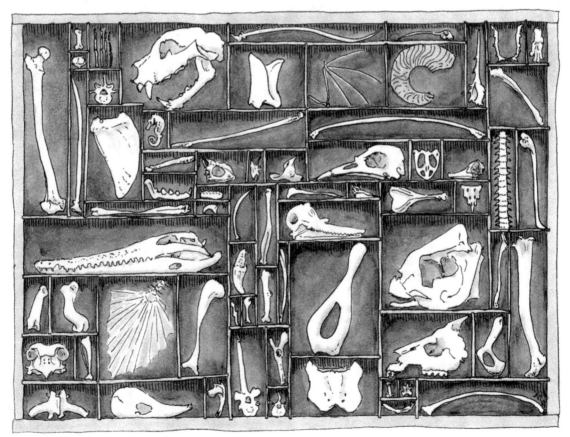

Angela Boyle

**ALL I HEARZ
ARE BELONG TO ME**

Kelly M. Ricker

Something to Crow About

by Anita K. Boyle

When I was a little kid, I thought chickens wore crowns on their heads.

SICILIAN BUTTERCUP

Every chicken is raised for a specific purpose. The Sicilian Buttercup is the one I admire most. Bred to produce eggs, it is a beautiful, medium-sized chicken. But Buttercups are unusual, too, since this is the only chicken on earth with a "cup comb." Unlike other chicken combs, this one has spikes like a normal "single comb," but it circles the head like a crown giving this chicken a royal stance. And they have green feet and legs, which is my favorite color. First thing every morning, our rooster crows sings a jazzy tune ending on a high note—a great way to start the day.

A Golden Hen

A Black & Yellow Chick

A Handsome Red Rooster

Which came first? Chicken or egg? Actually, the egg is the early bird! They were first "invented" (pun intended) by ancient reptiles during the Jurassic period. Maybe that's why many people think chickens look like domesticated dinosaurs.

With that age-old question out of the way, I would like to introduce a brand-spanking-new old wives tale about chicken eggs, which I've based entirely on empirical evidence. After hatching out many eggs in an incubator, it became evident that. . .

. . . the rounder the egg, the more likely it will become a hen upon hatching.

In the other hand, a pointy egg will usually become a rooster. I dare you to try it and see for yourself.

"The Dust Bowl"

RFORD 2018

Rachel Ford

Angela Boyle

Hatty Koerner

Melissa McGee

Melissa McGee

Farley Mowat
Canadian author
1921 - 2014

"We have doomed the wolf not
for what it is, but for what we
deliberately and mistakenly
perceive it to be –
the mythologized epitome of a
savage ruthless killer –
which is, in reality, no more
than a reflected image
of ourself."

David Humphreys

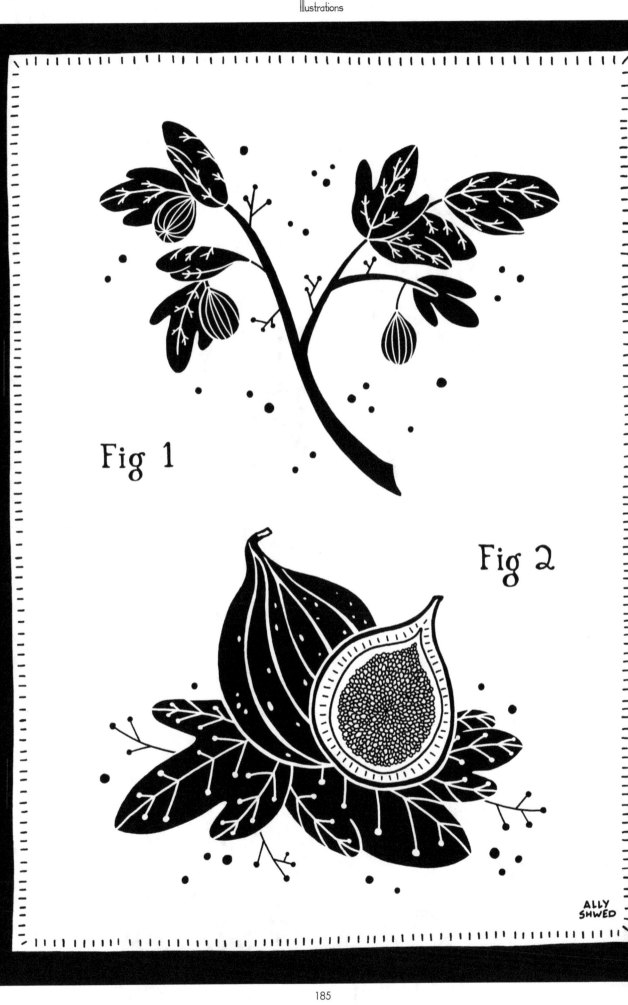

Fig 1

Fig 2

ALLY SHWED

Prickly Pear
Opuntia
engelmannii

Kami Koyamatsu

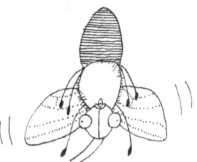

© Ej 2018 Elisa Järnefelt

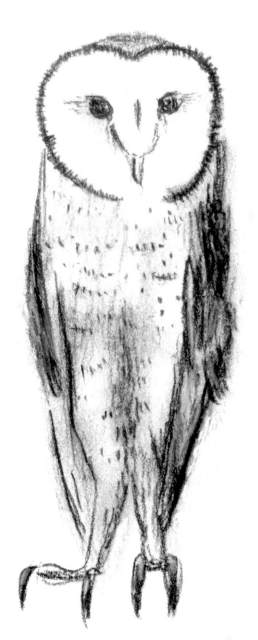

Moss Bastille

Angela Boyle

GRACE OLIVE WILEY

American Herpetologist

1884-1948

♂

♀

Lymantria dispar dispar

Alyssa Suzumura

ESMORC

Elise Smorczewski

K. Fraser
Kit Fraser

Liger

Pizzly Bear

Zebroid

Kit Fraser

Kely L Swann

David Kirkham

Moss Bastille

KOMODO
DRAGON
(*Varanus komodoensis*)

Native to Indonesian islands:
Komodo, Rintja,
Gillimontang, Flores,
and Padar

nipa palm

Komodos use
their tongue to
sense air particles as
their sense
of smell.

melati
(jasmine)

Melissa Capriglione

One-eyed Sphinx Moth

Nancy Canyon

PHOTOSYNTHETIC Animals

Eastern Emerald Elysia

This leaf shaped sea slug absorbs chloroplasts from the green algae that it eats. Special protein manufacturing genes allow the Eastern Emerald Elysia to keep the chloroplasts functional in its own cells so that it can photosynthesize energy.

Pea Aphid

Pea aphids may be white, orange or green in color. The color is the result of autonomously produced beta carotenoids in the aphid's body. These beta carotenoids allow orange and green aphids to produce ATP when exposed to sunlight.

Spotted Salamander

The spotted salamander has a symbiotic relationship with the Oophila amblystomatis algae. The algae lives inside the salamander's cells and creates a small amount of energy for the salamander using photosynthesis. This is most pronounced during the salamander's embryonic stage when eggs deprived of sunlight often fail to thrive.

SpottyLin 2018

Angela Boyle

Moss Bastille

The Shoebill and the Lungfish

Shoebills live in the freshwater swamps of Central Africa where African lungfish are plentiful. This large-billed, storklike bird will eat almost any aquatic creature——frogs, snakes, turtles, fish, and even baby crocodiles, but their all-time favorite meal is the lungfish. The lungfish can grow to six and a half feet long, while the shoebill can reach the height of a little more thatn four and a half feet. If that were the case, I'm not exactly sure who would eat whom.

Anita K. Boyle

Anita K. Boyle

Bernardo O. Dias

Kelly L. Swann

Elisa Järnefelt

Shashwat Mishra

Bibliographies

The Casual Carnivore by Hedj

Baskin, Leonid. "New World Deer (Capriolinae)." *Grzimek's Animal Life Encyclopedia*, 2nd edition, edited by Michael Hutchins, et al. Vol. 15: Mammals IV, Gale, 2004: 379–97. *Gale Virtual Reference Library*. Accessed November 3, 2017.

"Community Ecology." *Britannica Academic*, s.v. Accessed November 6, 2017. http://academic.eb.com/levels/collegiate/article/community-ecology/117280.

"Deer Eats Baby Bird." *YouTube* video, 1:23. Posted by "Linda Loo," May 16, 2010. https://www.youtube.com/watch?v=sQOQdBLHrLk.

Meckel, Lauren A., Chloe P. McDaneld, and Daniel J. Wescott. "White-Tailed Deer as a Taphonomic Agent: Photographic Evidence of White-Tailed Deer Gnawing on Human Bone." *Journal of Forensic Sciences* (May 2, 2017). doi:10.1111/1556-4029.13514.

"Nutrition." *Britannica Academic*, s.v. Accessed November 6, 2017. http://academic.eb.com/levels/collegiate/article/nutrition/108507.

"Rabbit Cannibalism." *Mississippi State University Extension Services*. Accessed November 10, 2017. http://extension.msstate.edu/content/rabbit-cannibalism.

Shackleton, David M. and Alton S. Harestad. "Bovids I: Kudus, Buffaloes, and Bison (Bovinae)." *Grzimek's Animal Life Encyclopedia*, 2nd edition, edited by Michael Hutchins, et al. Vol. 16: Mammals V, Gale, 2004: 11–25. *Gale Virtual Reference Library*. Accessed November 3, 2017.

Toon, Stephen, and Ann Toon. "Koalas (Phascolarctidae)." *Grzimek's Animal Life Encyclopedia*, edited by Michael Hutchins, et al. 2nd edition, Vol. 13: Mammals II, Gale, 2004, pp. 43–50. *Gale Virtual Reference Library*. Accessed November 3, 2017.

Wikipedia. "Filial Cannibalism." *Wikipedia*. Last modified October 26, 2017. https://en.wikipedia.org/wiki/Filial_cannibalism.

A Year in the Life by Kelly M. Ricker

Australian Koala Foundation. "Life Cycle of the Koala." Australian Koala Foundation, 2017. Last accessed December 1, 2017. https://www.savethekoala.com/about-koalas/life-cycle-koala.

San Diego Zoo Global. "Koala." San Diego Zoo: Animals & Plants, 2017. Last accessed on December 1, 2017. http://animals.sandiegozoo.org/animals/koala.

Wikipedia. "Koala." *Wikipedia*. Last modified November 13, 2017. https://en.m.wikipedia.org/wiki/Koala.

Puggle Life by Caitlin Hofmeister & Lauren Norby

Australian Associated Press. "Echidnas' 'Bizarre' Mating no Longer Obstacle to Successful Breeding Program." *The Guardian*, September 24, 2015. https://www.theguardian.com/world/2015/sep/24/echidnas-bizarre-mating-no-longer-obstacle-to-successful-breeding-program.

Morrow, Gemma and Stewart C. Nicol. "Cool Sex? Hibernation and Reproduction Overlap in the Echidna." *PLOS One* 4, no. 6 (2009): e6070. doi: 10.1371/journal.pone.0006070.

O'Niel, Dennis. "Echidna Reproduction." Classification of Living Things: An Introduction to the Principles of Taxonomy with a focus on Human Classification Categories. Last accessed January 26, 2018. https://www2.palomar.edu/anthro/animal/echidna_reproduction.htm.

Schneider, Nanette Yvette. "The Development of the Olfactory Organs in Newly Hatched Monotremes and Neonate Marsupials." *Journal of Anatomy* 219, no. 2 (August 2011): 229–42. doi:10.1111/j.1469-7580.2011.01393.x.

Street, Jacqui. "Echidnas' Unusual Mating Habits Revealed." ABC Science, January 11, 2011. http://www.abc.net.au/science/articles/2011/01/11/3110568.htm.

Rafflesia by Shing Yin Kohr

Shaw, Jonathan. "Colossal Blossom: Pursuing the Peculiar Genetics of a Parasitic Plant." *Harvard Magazine*. March/April 2017. https://harvardmagazine.com/2017/03/colossal-blossom.

Wilcox, Christie. "Parasitic Flower Pirates Genes from Its Host." Science Sushi. *Scientific American*. June 8, 2012. https://blogs.scientificamerican.com/science-sushi/parasitic-flower-pirates-genes-from-its-host.

The Shoebill by Bridget Comeau

BirdLife International. "*Balaeniceps rex*." The IUCN Red List of Threatened Species. Last modified 2016. doi:10.2305/IUCN.UK.2016-3.RLTS.T22697583A93622396.en.

Dodman, Tim. "Shoebill (*Balaeniceps rex*)." Widescreen Arkive. Last modified March 7, 2006. http://www.arkive.org/shoebill/balaeniceps-rex.

Montgomery, Sy. "Shoebill." *Encyclopedia Britannica*. Last modified November 5, 2017. https://www.britannica.com/animal/shoebill.

Steffen, Angie. "*Balaeniceps rex*, Shoebill." Animal Diversity Web. Last modified 2007. http://animaldiversity.org/accounts/Balaeniceps_rex.

A Salty Situation by Lisa Wolinsky & Melissa McGee

Ashish. "Why Can't Freshwater Fish Survive in Saltwater and Vice Versa?" Science ABC. Last modified February 2017. https://www.scienceabc.com/nature/animals/why-cant-freshwater-fish-survive-in-saltwater-and-vice-versa.html.

"Maintaining Water Balance 2: Osmoregulation in Fish." BBC. Last modified 2014. http://www.bbc.co.uk/bitesize/higher/biology/genetics_adaptation/maintaining_water_balance/revision/2.

"Why Do Some Fish Normally Live in Freshwater and Others in Saltwater? How Can Some Fish Adapt to Both?" *Scientific American*. Last modified 2017. https://www.scientificamerican.com/article/why-do-some-fish-normally.

Human Filter by Elisa Järnefelt

Atran, Scott and Douglas L. Medin. *The Native Mind and the Cultural Construction of Nature*. Cambridge, MA: MIT Press, 2008.

Boivin, Nicole. *Material Cultures, Material Minds: The Impact of Things on Human Thought, Society, and Evolution*. Cambridge, MA: University Press, 2008.

Coley, John D. and Kimberly Tanner. "Relations between Intuitive Biological Thinking and Biological Misconceptions in Biology Majors and Nonmajors." *CBE–Life Sciences Education* 14, no. 1 (March 2, 2015): 1–19. doi:10.1187/cbe.14-06-0094.

Cooper, William E., Jr. "Rapid Covering by Shadow as a Cue to Predation Risk in Three Lizard Species." *Behaviour* 146, no. 9 (2009): 1217–34. doi:10.1163/156853909X420008.

Dukas, Reuven. "Evolutionary Biology of Animal Cognition." *Annual Review of Ecology, Evolution, and Systematics* 35 (2004): 347–74. doi:10.1146/annurev.ecolsys.35.112202.130152.

Guthrie, Stewart Elliott. *Faces in the Clouds: New Theory of Religion*. New York: Oxford University Press, 1993.

Järnefelt, Elisa, Caitlin F. Canfield, and Deborah Kelemen. "The Divided Mind of a Disbeliever: Intuitive Beliefs about Nature as Purposefully Created among Different Groups of Non-Religious Adults." *Cognition* 140 (July 2015): 72–88. doi:10.1016/j.cognition.2015.02.005.

Kelemen, Deborah, Joshua Rottman, and Rebecca Seston. "Professional Physical Scientists Display Tenacious Teleological Tendencies: Purpose-Based Reasoning as a Cognitive Default." *Journal of Experimental Psychology: General* 142, no. 4 (November 2013): 1074–83. doi:10.1037/a0030399.

Nature Education. "Photosynthetic Cells." Scitable. 2014. Last accessed on November 16, 2017. http://www.nature.com/scitable/topicpage/photosynthetic-cells-14025371.

The Amphibians and Reptiles of the Black County

by David Kirkham

Hughes, Morgan. "A Provisional Atlas of Reptiles and Amphibians in Birmingham and the Black Country." Birmingham, England: The Wildlife Trust for Birmingham and the Black Country, 2005. http://www.bbcwildlife.org.uk/sites/birmingham.live.wt.precedenthost.co.uk/files/Reptile%20and%20Amphibian%20Atlas.pdf.

The Shark Lady by Kit Fraser

Clark, Eugenie, and Ann McGovern. *The Desert Beneath the Sea*. New York: Scholastic, 1991.

Eilperin, Juliet. "Eugenie Clark 'Shark Lady' Who Explored Ocean Depths, Dies at 92." *The Washington Post*, February 26, 2015. https://www.washingtonpost.com/national/health-science/eugenie-clark-shark-lady-whoexplored-ocean-depths-dies-at-92/2015/02/26/9c025be4-bd64-11e4-bdfa-b8e8f594e6ee_story.html.

Huggins, Amy. "Eugenie Clark, Ph.D. (1922–2015)." *Archives of Maryland*. February 26, 2015. http://msa.maryland.gov/megafile/msa/speccol/sc3500/sc3520/013500/013574/html/13574bio.html.

McGovern, Ann and Ruth Chew. *Shark Lady: True Adventures of Eugenie Clark*. New York: Scholastic, 1978.

Cute or Deadly: Llama Edition by Angela Boyle

Beckuis, Kim Knox. "Llama Facts: 22 Fun Facts about These Curious Creatures." TripSavvy. Posted May 16, 2017. https://www.tripsavvy.com/fun-facts-about-llamas-3880940.

Wikipedia. "Llama." *Wikipedia*. Last updated January 26, 2018. https://en.wikipedia.org/wiki/Llama.

Saliva and Skin by Stephen R. Bissette & Ross Wood Studlar

(Along with the footnoted news items)

American Museum of Natural History, *General Guide to the American Museum of Natural History*, Science Guide #118. New York: Man and Nature Publications: 1956: 111–12.

Lady Broughton. "A Modern Day Dragon Hunt on Komodo: An English Yachting Party Traps and Photographs the Huge and Carnivorous Dragon Lizard of the Lesser Sundas." *National Geographic Magazine* 70, no. 3 (September 1936: 321–33.

Burden, W. Douglas. *Dragon Lizards of Komodo: An Expedition to the Lost World of the Dutch East Indies*. G. P. Putnam's Sons, 1927.

———. "Stalking the Dragon Lizard on the Island of Komodo." *National Geographic Magazine* 52, no. 2 (August 1927): 216–32.

———. "Trapping the Man-Eating Dragon Lizards of Komodo." *The Literary Digest*, June 18, 1927.

Chung, Ezra M. C., Scott N. Dean, Crystal N. Propst, Barney M. Bishop, and Monique L. van Hoek. "Komodo Dragon-Inspired Synthetic Peptide DRGN-1 Promotes Wound-Healing of a Mixed-Biofilm Infected Wound." *Nature Partner Journal: Biofilms and Microbiomes* 3 (April 11, 2017). https://www.nature.com/articles/s41522-017-0017-2.

"Fort Worth Zoo Welcomes 11 Komodo Dragon Hatchlings." CBS-DFW, November 28, 2017. http://dfw.cbslocal.com/2017/11/28/fort-worth-zoo-komodo-dragon.

Goldner, Orville and George E. Turner, *The Making of KING KONG: The Story Behind a Film Classic*. New York: A. S. Barnes & Company, 1927: 37–40.

Hornaday, William T. *Official Guide Book to the New York Zoological Park, Komodo Dragon Edition*. New York Zoological Society, 1934.

Kern, James A. "Dragon Lizards of Komodo." *National Geographic Magazine* 134, no. 6 (December 1968): 872–80.

Lutz, Dick and J. Marie Lutz, *Komodo: The Living Dragon*. Salem, OR: Dimi Press, 1971.

Maestripieri, Dario. "Improbable Antics: Notes from a Gorilla Guru." In *King Kong Is Back!: An Unauthorized Look at One Humongous Ape*, edited by David Brin. Dallas, TX: Benbella Books, Inc, 2005: 85–91.

Morris, Ramona and Desmond Morris, *Men and Apes*. New York: McGraw-Hill Book Company, 1966.

Turner, George E., Orville Goldner, expanded and revised by Michael H. Price. *Spawn of Skull Island: The Making of King Kong*. Baltimore, MD: Luminary Press, 2002: 23–24.

Vertlieb, Steve. "The Man Who Saved King Kong." *The Girl in the Hairy Paw: King Kong as Myth, Movie, and Monster*, edited by Ronald Gottesman and Harry Geduld. New York: Avon Books, 1976: 30.

Wiley, Judy. "Dragons Invade Fort Worth Zoo (Baby Ones, That Is)." *Star-Telegram*, November 27, 2017. http://www.star-telegram.com/news/local/article186689283.html.

Are Zoos a Good Idea? by David Humphreys

"2016 Report Shows AZA-Accredited Zoos and Aquariums' Record-Breaking Contribution to Wildlife Conservation." Association of Zoos & Aquariums, September 27, 2017. https://www.aza.org/aza-news-releases/posts/2016-report-shows-aza-accredited-zoos-and-aquariums-record-breaking-contribution-to-wildlife-conserv.

Angier, Natalie. "Do Gorillas Even Belong in Zoos? Harambe's Death Spurs Debate." *The New York Times*, June 6, 2016. https://www.nytimes.com/2016/06/07/science/gorilla-shot-harambe-zoo.html.

Bekoff, Marc and Pierce, Jessica. "Are Zoo Animals Happy? There's a Simple Empathy Test We Can Apply." *Salon*, April 16, 2017. https://www.salon.com/2017/04/16/are-zoo-animals-happy-theres-a-simple-empathy-test-we-can-apply. From *The Animals' Agenda: Freedom, Compassion, and Coexistence in the Human Age*. Boston: Beacon Press, 2017.

Bryant, Charles, and Josh Clark. "Are Zoos Good or Bad for Animals?" How Stuff Works, April 8, 2010. https://www.stuffyoushouldknow.com/podcasts/are-zoos-good-or-bad-for-animals.htm.

Clubb, Ros, Marcus Rowcliffe, Phyllis Lee, Khyne U. Mar, Cynthia Moss, and Georgia J. Mason. "Compromised Survivorship in Zoo Elephants." *Science* 322, no. 5908 (December 12, 2008): 1649, doi:10.1126/science.1164298.

Francisco, Edna. "Zoo Carnivores Need More Space." *Science*, October 1, 2003. http://www.sciencemag.org/news/2003/10/zoo-carnivores-need-more-space.

Hone, David. "Why Zoos Are Good." *The Guardian*, August 19, 2014. https://www.theguardian.com/science/lost-worlds/2014/aug/19/why-zoos-are-good.

Morell, Virginia. "A Condor Crosses the Border." *Science*, April 10, 2007. http://www.sciencemag.org/news/2007/04/condor-crosses-border.

———. "Do Zoos Shorten Elephant Life Spans?" *Science*, December 11, 2008. http://www.sciencemag.org/news/2008/12/do-zoos-shorten-elephant-life-spans.

Wikipedia. "Zoo." *Wikipedia*. Last modified January 29, 2018. https://en.wikipedia.org/wiki/Zoo.

Ghost Slug by Salakjit

BBC News. "Worm-Eating Slug Found in Garden." *BBC News.* Last modified July 10, 2008. http://news.bbc.co.uk/2/hi/uk_news/wales/south_east/7498195.stm.

Grant, Caroline. "Alien 'Ghost Slug' Blazes Slimy Trail Through British Gardens." *Daily Mail.* July 9, 2008. http://www.dailymail.co.uk/news/article-1033864/Alien-Ghost-Slug-blazes-slimy-trail-British-gardens.html.

Mosco, Rosemary. "10 Slippery Facts About Slugs." *Mental Floss.* January 27, 2017. http://mentalfloss.com/article/91588/10-slippery-facts-about-slugs.

Owen, James. "Photo in the News: Flesh-Eating Slug Found in Wales." *National Geographic News.* July 16, 2008. https://news.nationalgeographic.com/news/2008/07/080716-slug-photo.html.

Rowson, Ben. "The Long Reach of the Ghost Slug." *National Museum Wales.* August 11, 2014. https://museum.wales/articles/2014-08-11/The-Long-Reach-of-the-Ghost-Slug.

Turbanov, Ilya and Igor Balashov. "A Second Record of *Selenochlamys* (Stylommatophora: Trigonochlamydidae) from Crimea." *Malacologica Bohemoslovaca* 14 (. January 15, 2005): 1–4. http://mollusca.sav.sk/pdf/14/14.Turbanov.pdf.

Turner, Robin. "Carnivorous Ghost Slug Is a New Species." *Wales Online.* Last modified March 29, 2013. https://www.walesonline.co.uk/news/wales-news/carnivorous-ghost-slug-new-species-2108145.

Wikipedia. "Ghost Slug." *Wikipedia.* Last modified February 16, 2018. https://en.wikipedia.org/wiki/Ghost_slug.

Acalyptrata by Alyssa Suzumura

Barber, K. N. "*Strongylophthalmyia pengellyi n. sp.*, A Second Species of Nearctic Strongylophthalmyiidae (Diptera)". Journal of the Entomological Society of Ontario 137 (2006): 81–109.

CSIRO Entomology. Anatomical Atlas of Flies. *Anatomical Atlas of Flies.* 2004. http://www.ento.csiro.au/biology/fly/flyGlossary.html.

Iowa State University Department of Entomology. *Bugguide.* Last accessed January 24, 2018. https://bugguide.net/node/view/15740.

Johnson, Norman F. and Charles A. Triplehorn. *Borror and Delong's Introduction to the Study of Insects*, 7th Edition. Pacific Grove, CA: Brooks Cole, 2004.

Mathis, W. N. and T. Zatwarnicki. "Revision of New World Species of the Shore-fly Subgenus Allotrichoma Becker of the Genus Allotrichoma with Description of the Subgenus Neotrichoma (Diptera, Ephydridae, Hecamedini)." Zookeys 2012, no. 161 (January 2012): 1–101. doi:10.3897/zookeys.161.201.

McAlpine, J. F., ed. *Manual of Nearctic Diptera*, Volume 2. Hull, Quebec, Canada: Minister of Supply and Services Canada, 1987.

Tofilski, Adam. *DrawWing.* 2008. Last accessed January 24, 2018. http://drawwing.org.

University of British Columbia Department of Zoology. Spencer Entomological Collection. Last accessed January 24, 2018. https://www.zoology.ubc.ca/~biodiv/entomology.

Wikipedia. "Helaeomyia petrolei." *Wikipedia.* Last modified January 13, 2018. https://en.wikipedia.org/wiki/Helaeomyia_petrolei.

The Ghost Owl by Bernardo O Dias

Machado, Filipa. Personal communication. 2017.

Marti, Carl D., Alan F. Poole, and Louis R. Bevier. "Barn Owl (*Tyto alba*)." Birds of North America. Last updated June 1, 2005. doi:10.2173/bna.1.

Wagner, Hermann, Matthia Weger, Michael Klaas, and Wolfgang Schröder. "Features of Owl Wings that Promote Silent Flight." *Interface Focus* 7, no. 1 (February 6, 2017): 20160078. doi:10.1098/rsfs.2016.0078.

Wikipedia. "Barn Owl." *Wikipedia.* Last modified November 20, 2017. https://en.wikipedia.org/wiki/Barn_owl.

Ä'äy Chu by Rachel Ford

Coutts, R. C. *Yukon Places and Names*, 2nd edition. Whitehorse, YT: Moose Creek Publishing, 2003.

Erickson, Jon. *Glacial Geology: How Ice Shapes the Land.* New York: Facts on File, 1996.

LaChapelle, Edward R. *Field Guide to Snow Crystals.* Seattle, WA: University of Washington Press, 1969.

Mary Jane Johnson, Heritage Manager, Kluane First Nation. Personal exchange, email. November 7, 2017.

Schwartz, John. "Climate Change Reroutes a Yukon River in a Geological Instant." *New York Times*, April 17, 2017. https://www.nytimes.com/2017/04/17/science/climate-change-glacier-yukon-river.html.

Shugar, Daniel H., John J. Clague, James L. Best, Christian Schoof, Michael J. Willis, Luke Copland, and Gerard H. Roe. "River Piracy and Drainage Basin Reorganization Led by Climate-Driven Glacier Retreat." *Nature Geoscience* 10 (April 2017): 370–76.

"Slims River." Yukon Geographical Place Names Board. Last accessed November 25, 2017. http://yukonplacenames.ca/?s=Slims+River.

Roots, Charles Frederick, C. A. Scott Smith, and J. C. Meikle, eds. *Ecoregions of the Yukon Territory: Biophysical Properties of Yukon Landscapes.* PARC Technical Bulletin No. 04-01. Summerland, BC: Agriculture and Agri-Food Canada, 2004.

Chicken Scratch by Elise Smorczewski

Barber, Joseph. *The Chicken: A Natural History.* New York: Race Point Publishing, 2012.

Damerow, Gail. *Storey's Guide to Raising Chickens: Care, Feeding, Facilities.* North Adams, MA: Storey Publishing, 2010.

Lawler, Andrew. *Why Did the Chicken Cross the World?: The Epic Saga of the Bird that Powers Civilization.* New York: Atria Books, 2016.

Staples, Tamara and Ira Glass. *The Magnificent Chicken: Portraits of the Fairest Fowl.* San Francisco, CA: Chronicle, 2013.

Montgomery, Sy. *Birdology: Adventures with a Pack of Hens, a Peck of Pigeons, Cantankerous Crows, Fierce Falcons, Hip Hop Parrots, Baby Hummingbirds, and One Murderously Big Living Dinosaur.* New York: Free Press, 2010.

Marino, Lori. "Thinking Chickens: A Review of Cognition, Emotion, and Behavior in the Domestic Chicken." *Animal Cognition* 20, no. 2 (March 2017): 127–47. doi:10.1007/s10071-016-1064-4.

Jaucourt, Louis, Chevalier de. "Sacred Chickens." *The Encyclopedia of Diderot & d'Alembert Collaborative Translation Project.* Translated by Dena Goodman. Ann Arbor: Michigan Publishing, University of Michigan Library, 2007. http://hdl.handle.net/2027/spo.did2222.0000.865. Accessed November 30, 2017. Originally published as "Poulets Sacrés." *Encyclopédie ou Dictionnaire raisonné des sciences, des arts et des métiers*, 13:203 (Paris, 1765).

Lawler, Andrew and Jerry Adler. "How the Chicken Conquered the World." *Smithsonian Magazine.* June 2012. https://www.smithsonianmag.com/history/how-the-chicken-conquered-the-world-87583657.

Special to *The New York Times*. "Egg Experiment in Space Prompts Questions." *New York Times.* March 30, 1989. Accessed November 30, 2017. http://www.nytimes.com/1989/03/31/us/egg-experiment-in-space-prompts-questions.html.

Smith, Roff. "Chicken DNA Challenges Theory that Polynesians Beat Europeans to Americas." *National Geographic.* March 19, 2014. https://news.nationalgeographic.com/news/2014/03/140318-polynesian-chickens-pacific-migration-america-science.

Ray, C. Claiborne. "How Many Eggs Does a Chicken Lay in Its Lifetime?" *New York Times.* April 18, 2016. https://www.nytimes.com/2016/04/19/science/how-many-eggs-does-a-chicken-lay-in-its-lifetime.html.

Hall, Ishbel, dir. "Chickens." *Private Life of . . . .* July 15, 2010.

Taking a Peek at the One-Eyed Sphinx Moth
by Anita K. Boyle

Burris, Judy and Wayne Richards. *The Secret Lives of Backyard Bugs: Discover Amazing Butterflies, Moths, Spiders, Dragonflies, and Other Insects!* North Adams, MA: Storey Publishing, 2011.

Eisele, Tim. "One-Eyed Sphinx Moth, with Eggs and Caterpillars and Pupa." The Backyard Arthropod Project. July 25, 2012. http://somethingscrawlinginmyhair.com/2012/07/25/one-eyed -sphinx-moth-with-eggs-and-caterpillars-and-pupa.

Gangwere, S.K. *Entomology*. Livonia, MI: First Page Publications, 2005.

Missouri Botanical Garden. "Metamorphosis." Butterfly School. Last modified 2016. http://www.butterflyschool.org/new/meta.html.

Pyle, Robert Michael. Personal emails. June 2017.

Raffles, Hugh, ed. *Insectopedia*. New York: Pantheon Books, 2010.

Watts, Barrie. *Moth*. Englewood Cliffs, NJ : Silver Burdett Press, 1990.

Wikipedia. "Moth." *Wikipedia*. Last modified November 26, 2017. https://en.wikipedia.org/wiki/Moth.

Wikipedia. "Sphingidae." *Wikipedia*. Last modified November 26, 2017. https://en.wikipedia.org/wiki/Sphingidae.

Bone Collector by Nancy Canyon

Gilbert, Stephen G. *Pictorial Anatomy of the Cat*. Seattle: University of Washington Press, 1968.

Huff, Paula Rogers. *Predator or Prey? Skull Characteristics*. Wisconsin 4-H Youth Development Program, 2017.

Kavanagh, James and Raymond Leung. *Animal Skulls and Bones: A Waterproof Pocket Guide to the Bones of Common North American Animals*. Waterford Press, 2010, 2016.

Liszewski, Erica. "Basic Animal Anatomy." Ellen Million Graphics, 2011. http://emg-zine.com/item.php?id=729.

"Website Index of Species." Will's Skull Page. Last accessed November 27, 2017. http://www.skullsite.co.uk/lists.htm.

The Woman without Fear by Spratty Lin

Fisher, Becky. "Female Entomologist: Grace Olive Wiley (1883–1948)." Tri-Trophic Thematic Collection Network. March 13, 2014. http://tcn .amnh.org/updates/femaleentomologistgraceolivewiley1883-1948.

Mannix, Daniel Pratt. "The Woman without Fear." In Herriot, James. *All Creatures Great and Small*. New York: McGraw-Hill, 1963.

Murphy, James B. and David E. Jacques. "Death from Snakebite: The Entwined Histories of Grace Olive Wiley and Wesley H. Dickinson." *Bulletin of the Chicago Herpetological Society*, 2006. http://www.chicagoherp.org/bulletin/41(Supplement).pdf.

Wikipedia. "Grace Olive Wiley." *Wikipedia*. Last updated November 6, 2017. https://en.wikipedia.org/wiki/Grace_Olive_Wiley.

Zoo Review. "Zoo History: The Lady and the Cobra." The Zoo Review, March 10, 2014. http://thezooreviewer.blogspot.com/2014/03/zoo -history-lady-and-cobra.html.

Animals that Eat Light by Kevin Kite & Michelle McCauley

Laetz, Elise M. J., Victoria C. Moris, Leif Moritz, André N. Haubrich, and Heike Wägele. "Photosynthate Accumulation in Solar-Powered Sea Slugs—Starving Slugs Survive Due to Accumulated Starch Reserves." *Frontiers in Zoology* 14 (January 19, 2017): 4. doi:10.1186/s12983-016-0186-5.

Leblang, Charlotte. "Zooxanthellae and Their Symbiotic Relationship with Marine Corals." *Microbewiki*. Last updated October 2, 2015. https://microbewiki.kenyon.edu/index.php/Zooxanthellae_and _their_Symbiotic_Relationship_with_Marine_Corals.

MacKenzie, Debora and Michael Le Page. "Eat Light: Dawn of the Plantimals." *New Scientist* 208, no. 2790 (December 11, 2010): 32–35. doi:10.1016/S0262-4079(10)63057-6.

Petherick, Anna. "A Solar Salamander." *Nature*. July 30, 2010. doi:10.1038/news.2010.384.

Rowland, Teisha. "First Known Photosynthetic Animal: Part Slug, Part Plant, Entirely Amazing." *Santa Barbara Independent*. January 30, 2010. https://www.independent.com/news/2010/jan/30/first -known-photosynthetic-animal.

Rumpho, Mary E., Karen N. Pelletreau, Ahmed Moustafa, and Debashish Bhattacharya. "The Making of a Photosynthetic Animal." *Journal of Experimental Biology* 214, no. 2 (2011): 303–11. doi:10.1242/jeb.046540.

Rumpho, Mary E., Elizabeth J. Summer, and James R. Manhart. "Solar-Powered Sea Slugs. Mollusc/Algal Chloroplast Symbiosis." *Plant Physiology* 123, no. 1 (May 2000): 29–38. doi:10.1104/pp.123.1.29.

Rumpho, Mary E., Jared M. Worful, Jungho Lee, Krishna Kannan, Mary S. Tyler, Debashish Bhattacharya, Ahmed Moustafa, and James R. Manhart. "Horizontal Gene Transfer of the Algal Nuclear Gene *psbO* to the Photosynthetic Sea Slug *Elysia chlorotica*." *PNAS* 105, no. 46 (November 18, 2008): 17867–71. doi:10.1073/pnas .0804968105.

Rybak, Sarah. "4 Incredible Photosynthetic Animals." University of Michigan Technology News. March 21, 2013. https://umich.uloop .com/news/view.php/77109/4-incredible-photosynthetic-animals.

Schanker, Gwendolyn. "It's an Animal! It's a Plant! No, It's an Amazing Acquired Phototroph!" *Oceanus Magazine* 52, no. 2 (Spring 2017): 26-28. https://www.whoi.edu/cms/files/17G0006 -Oceanus_v52n2-26-28_250965.pdf.

Venn, A. A., J. E. Loram, and A. E. Douglas. "Photosynthetic Symbioses in Animals." *Journal of Experimental Botany* 59, no. 5 (March 2008): 1069–80. doi:10.1093/jxb/erm328.

The Friendship Park Binational Garden by Ally Shwed

Watman, Dan. Interview by Ally Shwed. October 24, 2017.

Bad Luck Lemur by Moss Bastille

Boucher, Elizabeth. "*Daubentonia madagascariensis*, Aye-Aye." Animal Diversity Web. 2007. http://animaldiversity.org/accounts /Daubentonia_madagascariensis.

Duke University. "Aye-Aye: *Daubentonia madagascariensis*." Duke Lemur Center. Accessed November 16, 2017. http://lemur .duke.edu/discover/meet-the-lemurs/aye-aye.

Davies, Ella. "Aye-Aye lemur 'heats up' its special foraging finger." BBC Nature News. January 17, 2012. http://www.bbc.co.uk /nature/16577537.

Giancola, Heidi. "Aye-Aye, *Daubentonia madagascariensis*." New England Primate Conservancy. March 2016. http://www .neprimateconservancy.org/aye-aye.html.

Gron, Kurt. "Aye-Aye, *Daubentonia madagascariensis*." Primate Info Net, National Primate Research Center, University of Wisconsin. July 27, 2007. http://pin.primate.wisc.edu/factsheets/entry/aye-aye.

International Union for Conservation of Nature and Natural Resources. "*Daubentonia madagascariensis*." The ICUN Red List of Threatened Species. 2014. Last accessed November 16, 2017. http://www.iucnredlist.org/details/6302/0.

Simon, Matt. "Absurd Creature of the Week: Aye-Aye Gives World the Highly Elongated Finger." *Wired*. September 20, 2013. https://www.wired.com/2013/09/absurd-creature-of-the-week -aye-aye-gives-world-the-highlyelongated-finger.

Invasive Nomads by Kami Koyamatsu

Grupp, Susan. "Biology & Life Cycle." University of Illinois Extension Gypsy Moth Northeastern Illinois Reporting Site. Accessed November 9, 2017. https://extension.illinois.edu/gypsymoth /biology.cfm.

"Gypsy Moth." Gypsy Moth Program. September, 2017. Accessed November 9, 2017. https://agr.wa.gov/PlantsInsects/InsectPests ?GypsyMoth.

"Gypsy Moths." Mass Audubon. July 2016. Accessed November 9, 2017. https://www.massaudubon.org/learn/nature-wildlife/insects-arachnids/nuisance-moths/gypsy-moths.

Liebhold, Sandy. "E. Leopold Trouvelot, Perpetrator of our Problem." Gypsy Moth in North America. October 29, 2003. Accessed December 5, 2017. https://www.fs.fed.us/ne/morgantown/4557/gmoth/trouvelot.

Washington State Department of Agriculture, Plant Protection Division. *Gypsy Moth Program Survey Manual 2017*. Olympia, WA: Washington State Department of Agriculture, Laboratory Services Division, 2017.

Washington State Department of Agriculture, Plant Protection Division. *Gypsy Moth in Washington State: A Gypsy Moth Primer*. Olympia, WA: Washington State Department of Agriculture, 2011.

Fantasic Ficus, Full of Figs by Angela Boyle

Chandler, William Henry. *Deciduous Orchards: Illustrated with 109 Engravings*. Philadelphia: Lea and Febiger, 1942: 363–375.

Childers, Norman Franklin. *Modern Fruit Science: Orchard and Small Fruit Culture*, 7th edition. New Brunswick, NJ: Horticulture Publications, Rutgers University, 1976: 489–492.

Crase, John. "Fig Wasps Tavel Further Than Any Other Insect." Zoology, *The Guardian*. November 22, 2009. https://www.theguardian.com/science/2009/nov/23/fig-wasp-insect.

Crair, Ben. "Love the Fig." Elements, *The New Yorker* (August 10, 2016). https://www.newyorker.com/tech/elements/love-the-fig.

Druse, Ken. *Planthropology: The Myths, Mysteries, and Miracles of My Garden Favorites*. New York: Clarkson Potter Publishers, 2008.

Dumont, Elizabeth R., George D. Weiblen, and John R. Winkelmann. "Preferences of Fig Wasps and Fruit Bats for Figs of Functionally Dioecious *Ficus pungens*." *Journal of Tropical Ecology* 20 (2004): 233–238. doi:10.1017/S0266467403001147.

Johns, Leslie and Violet Stevenson. *Fruit for the Home and Garden: A Comprehensive Guide to Cultivation and Culinary Use*. North Ryde, Australia: Angus and Robertson Publishers, 1985: 115–119.

Shanahan, Mike. *Gods, Wasps and Stranglers: The Secret History and Redemptive Future of Fig Trees*. White River Junction, Vermont: Chelsea Green Publishing, 2016.

Sutton, David C. *Figs: A Global History*. London: Reaktion Books, 2014.

Farm to Bust by Hatty Koerner

Burns, Ken, dir. *The Dust Bowl*. Walpole, NH. Florintine Films: 2012. PBS distributed.

Colpitts, George, Shannon Stunden Bower, and Bill Waiser. "Climate and Change: Making Sense of the Dustbowl Years on the Canadian Prairies." *University of Saskatchewan*. Accessed on November 20, 2017. http://climateandchange.usask.ca/index.html.

Flood, Alison. "Melvyn Bragg Films John Steinbeck Documentary." *The Guardian*. May 18, 2011.

Leopold, Aldo. *Aldo Leopold's Southwest*. Eds. David E. Brown and Neil B. Carmony. Albuquerque: University of New Mexico Press, 1995.

Manning, Richard. *Grassland: The History, Biology, Politics, and Promise of the American Prairie*. New York: Penguin Books, 1997.

Worster, Donald. *Dust Bowl: The Southern Plains in the 1930s*. New York: Oxford University Press, 1979.

Haast's Eagle by Shashwat Mishra

Gill, Brian and Paul Martinson. *New Zealand's Extinct Birds*. Auckland, New Zealand: Random Century, 1991.

"Haast's Eagle / Pouakai." Prehistoric Wildlife. Last accessed November 2017. http://www.prehistoric-wildlife.com/species/h/haast%27s-eagle.html.

"Haast's Eagle." New Zealand Birds Online. Accessed November 2017. http://nzbirdsonline.org.nz/species/haasts-eagle#primary-specie.

"Monsters We Met: NEW ZEALAND HAASTS EAGLE." *YouTube* video, 2:55. Posted by "Luke Kendall," July 28, 2009. https://www.youtube.com/watch?v=H89iXWEKMMc.

Oliver, Walter Reginald Brook. *New Zealand Birds*. Wellington: A. H. and A. W. Reed, 1955.

Tennyson, Alan J. D. and Paul Martinson. *Extinct Birds of New Zealand*. Wellington: Te Papa Press, 2006.

My, What Hairy Ears You Have by Kelly L. Swann

"Caracal." Oregon Zoo. Last accessed December 1, 2017. https://www.oregonzoo.org/discover/animals/caracal.

"Caracal." San Diego Zoo. Last accessed December 1, 2017. http://animals.sandiegozoo.org/animals/caracal.

Skinner, John D., and Chimimba, Christian T. *The Mammals of the Southern African Subregion*. Cape Town, South Africa: Cambridge University Press, 2005.

Ligers and Other Hybrids by Tom O'Brien

Boulenger, Edward George, and Herbert George Wells. *World Natural History*. London: Batsford, 1937.

Dumor, Komla. "Siberian Zoo Breeds the World's First Liliger." BBC News. September 18, 2012. http://www.bbc.com/news/av/world-europe-19633192/siberian-zoo-breeds-the-world-s-first-liliger.

"Genetic Pollution: The Great Genetic Scandal." Institute for Agriculture and Trade Policy. July 22, 2002. https://www.iatp.org/news/genetic-pollution-the-great-genetic-scandal.

Guggisberg, C. A. W. *Wild Cats of the World*. New York: Taplinger Publishing, 1975.

"Hybrid." *Merriam-Webster*. Last accessed November 29, 2017. https://www.merriam-webster.com/dictionary/hybrid.

Jauregui, Andres. "Hercules, 922-Pound Liger, Is the World's Largest Living Cat (PHOTOS)." *The Huffington Post*. September 13, 2013. https://www.huffingtonpost.com/2013/09/13/hercules-liger-worlds-largest-cat-photos_n_3920158.html.

"Ligers." Messybeast Portal. Accessed November 29, 2017. http://messybeast.com/genetics/hyb-liger.htm.

"Ligers: Info and Facts." The Liger: Meet the World's Largest Cat. Accessed November 29, 2017. http://ligerfacts.org.

Runge, Marschall Stevens and Cam Patterson, eds. *Principles of Molecular Medicine*. Totowa, New Jersey: Humana Press, 2006: 58.

"Tigon (Tion, Tigron, Tiglon)." Messybeast Portal. Accessed November 29, 2017. http://messybeast.com/genetics/hyb-tigon.htm.

Wricke, Gunter and Eberhard Weber. *Quantitative Genetics and Selection in Plant Breeding*. New York: Walter de Gruyter, 1986: 257.

Farley and the Wolves by Laura Martin
(In order of appearance within the comic)

Austen, Ian. "Farley Mowat, Author, Dies at 92; a Champion of the Far North." *New York Times*. May 7, 2014. https://www.nytimes.com/2014/05/08/world/americas/farley-mowat-canadian-writer-and-wildlife-advocate-dies-at-92.html.

Parini, Jay. "Farley Mowat Obituary." *The Guardian*. May 8, 2014. https://www.theguardian.com/environment/2014/may/08/farley-mowat.

Young, Ryan. "Farley Mowat and His Connection to Animals." *YouTube* video, 5:44. Posted by '999999999Vision," May 11, 2015. Originally recorded in 2005. https://www.youtube.com/watch?v=DXnnFT2pe20&t=121s.

Goddard, John. "A Real Whopper." *Saturday Night*, May 1996. http://tarekfatah.com/john-goddard-on-marley-fowat.

Nock, Ban. "Never Cry Wolf—A Pack of Lies." *Daily Kos*, December 9, 2012. https://www.dailykos.com/stories/2012/12/9/1168554/-Never-Cry-Wolf-A-Pack-of-Lies.

Northumberland News. "Farley Mowat's Works and Awards." *Northumberland News,* May 7, 2014. https://www.northumberlandnews.com/news-story/4505959-farley-mowat-s-works-and-awards.

Mowat, Farley. *Never Cry Wolf.* New York: Back Bay Books, 2001. Chapter 1, pg 10; Chapter 1, pg 15; Chapter 3, pgs 28–34; Chapter 9, pgs 91–94; Chapter 10, pgs 106–7; Chapter 11, pgs 112 16; Chapter 22, pgs 222–28; Chapter 12, pg 125; Chapter 12, pg 128; Preface, viii.

"Never Cry Wolf." IMDB. http://www.imdb.com/title/tt0086005.

Yellowstone Staff. "Wolf Reintroduction Changes Ecosystem." *My Yellowstone Park,* June 2, 2011. https://www.yellowstonepark.com/things-to-do/wolf-reintroduction-changes-ecosystem.

Borrell, Brendan. "Why Does Sarah Palin Support Shooting Wolves in Alaska?" *Scientific American,* February 6, 2009. https://www.scientificamerican.com/article/palin-shooting-wolves.

Coyne, Amanda. "Palin and the Wolves: Inside Alaska's Aerial Hunt." *Newsweek,* April 9, 2009. http://www.newsweek.com/palin-and-wolves-inside-alaskas-aerial-hunt-77305.

CBC News. "Wolf Cull Will See Animals Shot from Helicopter to Save B.C. Caribou." *CBC News,* January 15, 2015. http://www.cbc.ca/news/canada/british-columbia/wolf-cull-will-see-animals-shot-from-helicopter-to-save-b-c-caribou-1.2904364.

MacKinnon, J.B. "No One's Afraid of the Big, Bad Wolf—And That's the Problem" *Smithsonian Magazine,* October 23, 2017. https://www.smithsonianmag.com/science-nature/can-wolves-and-humans-coexist-180965337.

Pynn, Larry. "Pacific Rim National Park Reserve Visitors Urged to Keep Distance from Wolf Pack Showing Little Fear of People." *Vancouver Sun,* January 28, 2014. http://www.vancouversun.com/technology/Pacific+National+ Park+Reserve+visitors+urged+keep+distance+from+wolf+pack+showing+little/9436249/story.html.

Bob-Bobwhite by Melissa Capriglione

"Bobwhite Quail." *Indiana Department of Natural Resources.* 2017. https://www.in.gov/dnr/fishwild/3379.htm.

Brennan, Leonard A. "Northern Bobwhite." Cornell Lab of Ornithology: Birds of America. September 9, 2014. Last accessed December 1, 2017. https://birdsna.org/Species-Account/bna/species/norbob/introduction.

"Quail Posts—Sounds a Quail Makes—Texas Wildlife Association." *YouTube* video, 10:00. Posted by "Texas Wildlife Association," May 5, 2010. Accessed December 1, 2017. https://www.youtube.com/watch?v=mp6E9s5up6Y.

Angela Boyle

Index

Shashwat Mishra

Biographies

Moss Bastille is a graduate of The Center for Cartoon Studies. His work often focuses on nature and social isolation, a product of growing up in rural New England. He misses the ocean terribly.
moth-ire.tumblr.com
mbastille@coa.edu

Stephen R. Bissette was born in Vermont, 1955. Drawing by four, he made his first comic at eight. He sold *ABYSS* in 1977, was a pro by 1978. Retired as of 1999, he created *Tyrant* and has taught at CCS since 2005.
srbissette.com

Angela Boyle is a natural science illustrator, cartoonist, and editor. Her favorite animals are Brazilian tapirs and corgis. She wants a corgi-sized tapir.
AngelaBoyle.FlyingDodoStudio.com
angela@flyingdodopublications.com

Anita K. Boyle swirls the environment around in her art, whether as paper, an assemblage, or a poem. She is a *cum laude* graduate of art and English from Western Washington University.
egressstudio.com
anitakboyle@flyingdodostudio.com

Nancy Canyon holds an MFA in creative writing from Pacific Lutheran University and a certificate in fiction writing from the University of Washington. She has a visual communication degree from NW School of Art.
www.nancycanyon.com
nancy@nancycanyon.com

Melissa Capriglione is a comic artist and a nature hobbyist who loves birds and is passionate about preserving the environment. She learned about the northern bobwhite quail while working at a zoo.
mcapriglioneart.weebly.com
mcapriglione3995@gmail.com

Bridget Comeau. Gnome Queen enthusiastic about mushrooms. Loves all fantasy and Fae-folk. CCS class of 2015.
bridgetcomeau.tumblr.com
bridgetcomeau@gmail.com

Bernardo O. Dias. Art and science enthusiast. Also fantasy.
bernardoodias.wordpress.com
bernardood@gmail.com

Kit Fraser is an cartoonist living in New York. Her work can be found on *The Nib*, *The Stranger*, and in other publications and anthologies.
kitfraser.com
kitkfraser@gmail.com

Rachel Ford lives in the Yukon Territory of Canada and is surrounded by mountains and boreal forest. She and her partner met in the Slim's Valley two years before the river rerouted. They have two dogs.
www.rfordcomics.com
rfordcomics@gmail.com

Hedj, born and raised in New York, is a recent graduate from The Center for Carton Studies, loves the outdoors, and is very food motivated.
vesparts.tumblr.com
primitiverobot@gmail.com

Caitlin Hofmeister is a writer and filmmaker who makes videos and podcasts for the internet. She lives and works in Missoula, Montana.

David Humphreys is a cartoonist and a photographer. He is a Center for Cartoon Studies graduate who currently lives in Prague.
dbhum.com
dbhumphreys@gmail.com

Elisa Jarnefelt is Vermont-based illustrator and researcher. Her drawings are inspired both by observations in her family life as well as her research in the area of human cognition and nature.
www.instagram.com/aslittlecookingaspossible
simpledrawings@gmail.com

David Kirkham is a freelance writer and cartoonist whose work has featured in *Forbidden Planet*, *Awesome 'Possum*, and the *Desert Island Discs Fanzine*. He is the author of the graphic novel *Tripped Electric*.
www.facebook.com/DaveyDoodlebug
trippedelectric@gmail.com

Kevin Kite and Michelle McCauley create the science and culture comic *HURRY UP PLEASE IT'S TIME*. They live in the green hills of Vermont with two kids, two cats, some skunks, and several thousand bees.
hurryuppleaseitstime.com
klk@gmavt.net

Hatty Koerner focuses her artistic energy on drawing the natural world for children, and for the child inside each adult. Her artistic inspirations revolve around deviation; moss on roofs, mildew, spiky object, and scat.
hattythespider.net

Shing Yin Khor is an installation artist and cartoonist. She enjoys gently poking slugs.
sawdustbear.com
shingkohr@gmail.com

Kami Koyamatsu is a natural science illustrator and hopes to use her art to motivate conservation efforts by piquing people's interests in nature.

    kamikoyamatsu.com
    kamikoyamatsu@gmail.com

Laura Martin is a graduate of The Center for Cartoon Studies. Much like the caribou, the wolf has made her strong.

    lauramartinartist.tumblr.com
    laura.martin.artist@gmail.com

Melissa McGee is an artist with an insatiable love for learning, and an irrepressible need to create, be it art, comics, costumes, or a nice cup of tea.

    alchemist-and-druid.tumblr.com
    alchemist.and.druid@gmail.com

Shashwat Mishra is an artist currently working freelance. He's trying to figure life out in India. He lives with two cats.

    shashmishra.tumblr.com
    shashcomics@gmail.com

Lauren Norby is an artist and storyteller making comics, videos, and music. He lives in Missoula, Montana, USA.

    l-t-n.tumblr.com
    laurennorby@gmail.com

Tom O'Brien is a freelance cartoonist and illustrator living in upstate New York. He is currently working on a nonfiction graphic novel about the history of the world's most popular liquors.

    tomobriencomics.com
    tomobriencomics@gmail.com

Kelly M. Ricker is of a nerdy persuasion with a deep love for Star Wars and all things animated. She is an artist for mobile games and often babysits her sister's three dogs.

    artofkmricker.tumblr.com
    kmricker@gmail.com

Salakjit was born in Bangkok, Thailand, and raised in Queens, New York. She is a cartoonist, illustrator, and printmaker. When she's not making art, she enjoys reading, sleeping, and eating spicy food.

    salakjitcomix.tumblr.com

Ally Shwed is a cartoonist from New Jersey. Her work appears regularly in the Boston Globe and on *The Nib*, and she coruns Little Red Bird Press.

    Allyshwed.com
    Ally.shwed@gmail.com

Elise Smorczewski grew up on a farm that fostered a lifelong fascination with animals of all kinds. Nonfiction comics are a way to share that love.

    esmorc.tumblr.com
    esmorc@gmail.com

Spratty is a cartoonist living near Philadelphia with their various human companions, two snakes, and two cats. They think reptiles are pretty great.

    spratty-duck.com
    sprattyduckarts@gmail.com

Ross Wood Studlar became a fan of both Spider-Man and Ranger Rick when he was four. Today he still draws comics and is a park ranger at national parks.

    rosswoodstudlar.blogspot.com
    rwoodstudlar@gmail.com

Alyssa Suzumura is an entomologist and illustrator currently in graduate school at the University of Hokkaido in Japan. After identifying insects for the University of Washington for six years, she is now studying coastal beetle systematics. She spends a lot of time drawing beetle penises for identification purposes.

    alsuzumura.tumblr.com
    asuzu5@gmail.com

Kelly L. Swann has a keen interest for telling people's (and animal's) stories, and she's found comics to be her favorite medium.

    kellylswann.com
    klswann@gmail.com

Lisa Wolinsky is a writer of science, horror, romance, and corporate documentation. She keeps a dozen different hobbies for when one of them gets boring.

    alchemist-and-druid.tumblr.com
    alchemist.and.druid@gmail.com

Jon Chad (introduction author) teaches production at The Center for Cartoon Studies. He is also the creator of *Leo Geo* and *Volcanoes: Fire and Life* (First Second, 2016).

    jonchad.com

Tillie Walden (cover artist) is a cartoonist and illustrator from Austin, Texas. She is the creator of the Eisner-nominated webcomic *On a Sunbeam* as well as the recently published graphic memoir *SPiNNiNG*.

    www.tilliewalden.com

CPSIA information can be obtained
at www.ICGtesting.com
Printed in the USA
LVHW011549240820
663952LV00010B/515